# The Church Unleashed

## Frank R. Tillapaugh

D0111963

Regal Books

A Division of GL Publications
Ventura, CA U.S.A.

The translation of all Regal books is under the direction of GLINT.
GLINT provides technical help for the adaptation, translation and
publishing of books for millions of people worldwide. For information
regarding translation contact: GLINT, P.O. Box 6688, Ventura, California 93006.

Third Printing, 1983

Published by Regal Books
A Division of GL Publications
Ventura, California 93006
Printed in U.S.A.

**Library of Congress Cataloging in Publication Data**
Tillapaugh, Frank R.
    The Church unleashed.

    Includes bibliographical references.
    1. Church renewal.   2. Pastoral theology.   3. Bear Valley Bap-
    tist Church.   4. Tillapaugh, Frank R.
I. Title.
BV600.2.T54    1982          259          82-9783
ISBN 0-8307-0823-5                         AACR2

# Contents

# Foreword

Bear Valley Baptist Church is a plain, unimpressive building on a major Denver through street. Sandwiched in between two other churches, it lacks any pretense of imposing, typically ecclesiastical architecture. Outside it doesn't have a large parking area, and inside its facilities are surprisingly meager and cramped. But that building isn't really Bear Valley Baptist Church. That's merely the place where this church assembles. It's the operational base for the over 1,000 people who are Bear Valley Baptist Church, people who have been carrying on a remarkable, dynamic witness in a mushrooming metropolis. Bear Valley Baptist Church is a fellowship of believers, a fellowship that has been moving beyond the walls of a building, a fellowship that has shaken off its shackles and is now reaching out into areas of need and seizing opportunities to help in the name of Jesus Christ. It's a fellowship that within ten years has been transformed from a small, stagnant in-group into a pulsating task force of vision, service, enthusiasm, and growth.

The human catalyst of Bear Valley Baptist Church is one of my former students, Pastor Frank Tillapaugh. I must honestly say that in seminary he was not much of a bookworm! I must also say that he is not a scintillating pulpiteer. Neither is he a high-powered salesman nor an adroit administrator. No, Frank is a man who has a passion to be an agent of the Holy Spirit in unleashing the potential of God's people, the suppressed energy and creativity of the so-called laity. He is a man with the courage to be unconventional, innovative, experimental, abandoning tradition and shattering the shell of custom and conventionality. He is a man who has the gift of infecting others with his own dynamic concept of what Christianity is all about.

As Pastor Frank sees American evangelicalism today, many churches are introverted, concerned about attracting larger and larger congregations to their pulpit-centered services, increasing their budgets, improving and expanding their facilities while their members remain afflicted with arthritic spectatoritis. So, under God, Frank has been working at Bear Valley to reverse that whole process—and he has done so with dramatic results. His message, therefore, is clear and simple: unleash the church! Forget about bringing people in. Focus on getting God's people out where there are sin and pain and need. Forget about institutional success. Focus on outgroup service. Forget about binding members to an organization with ties of loyalty, cords of convivial programming, and busy intramural involvement. Focus on unshackling members, motivating them to give time and energy beyond any ecclesiastical ghetto.

Forget about growth as an end in itself. And, para-doxically, growth will take place as the by-product of a ministry which refuses to be self-centered and self-serving.

Frank is keenly aware that situations and personalities differ radically. He knows that in all God's kingdom there is no duplicate of Bear Valley, nor can there be. He knows that not all concepts and methods are transferable. But he likewise knows that many are. That is why he has told the Bear Valley story and told it with down-to-earth specifics. He has told it in the prayerful hope that like Bear Valley many churches elsewhere will become blessedly unshackled.

Vernon C. Grounds

# Part I
# The Strategy

During the 1970s Bear Valley Baptist Church grew. In 1970 there were about 100 active people in the church; by 1982 there were over 1,000. In 1970 the total income of the church was $16,763; ten years later it was over half-a-million dollars. That is significant growth, but it is not spectacular for a city church. Many churches can point to bigger statistics during a similar time period.

While statistical growth is an important theme in *The Church Unleashed*, it is not the major theme. The major theme is a certain philosophy of church ministry. Far more important than the fact that Bear Valley grew is the way it grew. The church has remained in small facilities—the sanctuary seats 275—while building a major ministry extending across the city of Denver. Bear Valley has developed a reputation for carrying on numerous ministries not normally found in the local church. The best way to describe what has happened is to say that the church has been unleashed.

Recently a student from Southwestern Theological Seminary spent several months traveling throughout the country visiting churches involved in ministries not usually found in the local church. When he returned to the seminary he published his findings in a small booklet for distribution to his classmates. He found many churches talking about renewal, new ministries, and a ministering laity; but talking was not doing. He concluded that Bear Valley was actively engaged in carrying out more different ministries than any of the other churches he visited. In the following pages I want to share some of the principles that have unleashed Bear Valley into ministries with street people, refugees, artists, international students, mothers of preschoolers, ex-convicts, and delinquent girls, to mention a few of the target groups.

Throughout this book the concept of the church unleashed into the community is set over and against the "fortress church." The fortress church puts up its building, starts its programs and concentrates primarily within its walls. The church unleashed is not unconcerned with what goes on within its church buildings, but it is only partially focused there. In the church unleashed an individual's primary ministry may be within one of many traditional church programs such as Sunday School. But there is an equal chance that his ministry may be in a prison or working with a foreign student. In either case, the norm is people-oriented ministry.

Of course, the categories of the church unleashed and the fortress church are not absolutes. Nevertheless, churches can be characterized by these terms. The contention of this book is that the overwhelming majority of evangelical churches are fortress-type churches. But our times call for just the opposite. The majority of our churches should be unleashed, ministering effectively throughout the great cities of this country.

We need the kind of people who joined David in 1 Chronicles 12. Here those who "came to David at Hebron to turn Saul's kingdom over to him" (v. 23) are described. Many noteworthy men are mentioned. "Men of Judah,. . . warriors ready for battle." Famous men of Ephraim came, as did experienced soldiers prepared for battle, with undivided loyalty, from Zebulun (see vv. 24-33).

In the midst of this list emphasizing bravery, loyalty and military skill comes the description of the "men of Issachar who *understood the times* and knew what Israel should do" (v. 32, italics added). We desperately need some modern men of Issachar in our churches. While some churches are obviously enjoying God's blessing, others are languishing. For every alive-and-growing evangelical church, I can point to five that are just the opposite. The situation is serious.

The principles discussed in *The Church Unleashed* were not found inscribed in stone on top of Mount Sinai. They are fallible; they certainly are not the final word on unleashing the church. I am convinced, however, that these principles are in tune with both Scripture and the needs of today's cities. Therefore, I believe they represent the kind of qualities David found among the men of Issachar. They are not exhaustive but perhaps they will make some contribution to those laboring to reach this generation for Christ, especially those in the local churches of our nation's cities.

# Chapter 1

# Needed: A Happy Marriage

I sat one evening in the living room of a middle-aged couple and hurt for them. As a pastor involved in the ministry of visitation I had visited hundreds of homes over the past eleven years and had enjoyed meeting new people on "their own turf." But early in my ministry I learned that these visits could be painful. Unfortunately, this couple's story had become familiar. This was the first time I had heard their particular version but the basic theme was an old one.

They had visited Bear Valley while searching for a new church home. Though they had hung on in their last church for as long as they thought they could, they felt guilty about leaving. It's always a delicate task not to gossip about a church you are leaving while at the same time explaining why you're looking for a new church.

As they reflected on their past church experiences there was little joy or satisfaction. Looking back over a period stretching across three decades, it had been a desperate grind. They had served on endless committees that never seemed to accomplish much. They had watched pastors come and go. They had seen the churches level out in attendance, hold their own and then go into decline. For some time they had been discouraged and disillusioned about the potential of the local church. But dropping out altogether was not an option for this highly committed couple. So they had reluctantly become involved in the distasteful task of "church shopping."

Their recollection of the past was not all doom and gloom. There had been good Sunday School classes, good ministries with youth and a lot of good friends over the years. But the element of the dynamic aliveness that comes from involvement in meaningful ministry was, for the most part, lacking. So much of the church-related work seemed trivial. Hours had been poured into decisions concerning buildings and parking lots. They had spent so much time discussing church business, and yet had invested little in people.

Their discouragement with the church was heightened by an experience the man had with a parachurch organization.[1] For a few years he was part of a dynamic chapter of the Christian Businessmen's Committee. His face lit up as he recalled how they had prayed together and how they had reached businessmen with the gospel. He described a genuine "front-line" ministry, one that took place out in his world—the business world. He had never had a comparable experience in the local church.

## An Old, Old Story

His glowing account of parachurch ministry was not surprising. I frequently hear similar stories. People often tell me about years of ministry and spiritual growth with Women's Bible Clubs, the Navigators, Inter-Varsity, Campus Crusade, Youth for Christ, etc. These exciting, rewarding experiences are often set alongside the dull, going-through-the-motions routine in a local church.

This couple, like so many I'd talked with, were discouraged. Their children had grown and left home. They could have just settled back and joined the electronic church. But they wanted to become part of a healthy, local body of believers.

After talking with people all over the greater Denver area, I know this couple is not unusual. Not long ago another man I talked with literally shook with anger and despair as he recalled the unsatisfactory situation in his last church. And, of course, the hurt isn't restricted merely to the laity. Southern Baptists have found that a pastoral crisis occurs about every eighteen months of ministry. An interesting corollary is that Southern Baptist pastors move on the average of every eighteen to twenty months. In the Alliance Church, the average pastor stays only between three and four years.[2] Pastors are not leaving just because God has called them to another ministry. They are leaving because they are discouraged. Within a short time a pastor feels, "I have taken this church as far as I can," which means the church is about where it was when he came, or maybe in a worse condition. Today, in my opinion, it takes at least five years to build any kind of significant ministry in a local church. But few pastors are staying in a church that long.

## What Is Happening in Our Churches?
The local church is the source of discouragement and disillusionment for scores of lay people

and pastors alike. Through the years, I have become acquainted with dozens of young people preparing for the ministry. I've had the privilege of teaching at a Bible college, a seminary and in summer training programs. In addition, over the past nine years, Bear Valley has become home for hundreds of students. Many of these students fear the church. They are afraid it will box them in, inhibit their creativity, place too many role expectations on them, expecting them to oil the machine and make the programs move. The percentage of students who are pessimistic about the possibilities of the local church is already far too high. The percentage of pastors and lay people who are pessimistic about the local church is also becoming far too high.

*The great evangelical power shift.* In an article in *Eternity* magazine entitled, "The Great Evangelical Power Shift," Stephen Board states, "In influence and in money—that is, in *power*—the parachurch agencies are running away with the ballgame."[3] That's a powerful assertion. It describes the feelings I experienced recently while attending a pastors' conference at the headquarters of Campus Crusade for Christ. We heard from Crusade's overseas directors. One after another these high-powered men of unusual dedication and ability described what God was doing in their part of the world. They described tremendous accomplishments as well as great expectations for the future.

We learned that Crusade's overseas missionary staff, serving in 50 countries, grew from 9,000 to over 11,000 last year. This figure represents full-time and associate staff members. (Compare this with the largest denominational mission force of just over 3,000 belonging to the Southern Baptists.) In addition, Crusade shared a vision of establishing some 2,500 "Here's Life" training centers around the world.

Campus Crusade's president, Bill Bright, told how he had once prayed for the salvation of one friend. Then he prayed for the salvation of his parents, then for a small group of students. God honored these requests and he began to pray for hundreds, then thousands, then millions, and now he and his co-workers at Campus Crusade are asking God for the salvation of billions of people. He went on to share that they had recently purchased a 5,000-acre site. Four thousand acres were to be sold for development; the remaining thousand would become the campus of a large Christian graduate school. On top of all this, Crusade had launched a campaign to raise a billion dollars to fund their ministries.

The message at Arrowhead Springs was clear. Campus Crusade is serious about the Great Commission. Shortly after that trip I attended a regional denominational meeting. The difference was like the difference between night and day. Instead of an atmosphere of "How can we win the world for Christ?" it was more like, "How can we hang on for another year?"

*What has happened on the evangelical scene since the 1940s?* Perhaps we need to back off a bit and ask why the great evangelical power shift has taken place. Parachurch ministries have been around for a long time; some would argue that they go back to the New Testament. But most of the best known and most active organizations have come into existence since the late 1930s. Inter-Varsity is the oldest of a long and impressive list including the Navigators, Campus Crusade for Christ, Youth for Christ, Young Life, International

Students, Inc., Child Evangelism, Teen Challenge, Jews for Jesus, Fellowship of Christian Athletes, plus dozens of others. Why have so many of these types of organizations come into existence in the past forty years?

The answer to that question is one of growing debate. I believe the primary positive reason is that God has raised them up. He has called the leadership, given the vision, provided the workers and finances. But what about the negative reasons? Again I quote Stephen Board: "The organizations, of which there are some 6,500 counting both Protestant and Catholic, will retort that they are merely 'arms of the church,' specialists helping the church do its job. They may privately add that they are simply doing what churches ought to be doing were they not so hidebound, disorganized, and pre-occupied with buildings."[4]

Back in the early forties, God gave Dawson Trotman a burning desire to reach sailors for Christ. Out of his ministry came the present-day worldwide ministry of the Navigators. It's not shameful that Trotman founded the Navigators. In fact, the entire evangelical community can rejoice that this superb ministry came into being. It is regrettable, however, that Trotman *had* to bypass the church to have an effective ministry with sailors. It wasn't possible to minister to sailors in the majority of local churches in the 1940s nor is it possible today. This raises a serious question: Why must people bypass the church to minister to many of the groups in our culture?

*Most churches are focused exclusively on the middle-class family.* Following World War II, a growing economy and expanding suburbia produced a middle-class boom. The increasingly powerful middle-class family unit became the almost exclusive focus of the white evangelical church. Churches either built in suburbia or they relocated there.

Church programs were, and still are, structured around the middle-class family unit. Some time ago, the *Home Mission* magazine of the Southern Baptist Convention lamented that over ninety percent of their churches were ministering nearly exclusively to a middle class which makes up about one-third of our cities.

To illustrate this point, you might try this little experiment sometime. Ask church people what they think of when you mention the church and its ministries. The vast majority of answers will fall within a very narrow range including, preaching, Sunday School, choir, children's and ladies' auxiliaries and youth programs. Don't anticipate answers such as street people, ex-convicts, prisoners, sailors, unchurched high school kids or members of the cults. Ministries that do not fit neatly into the middle-class scheme have simply been ignored.

When Dawson Trotman wanted to reach sailors, he realized the church was hopelessly turned inward. So he bypassed it.

In the 1980s, the middle-class heyday as we knew it in the forties and fifties, is over. If it was a mistake for the church to become too preoccupied with the middle class in the forties, it is an even bigger mistake today. Groups of people abound who do not neatly fit into the middle class. If we are to reach these people we must develop specialized target-group ministries.

It is not shameful that in the past four decades God has raised up a large number of parachurch organizations and blessed them with tremendous success. But it is regrettable that so few churches have broken out of their suburban, middle-class captivity. It is a shame that the only way the Lord has to reach numerous target groups has been by raising up specialized ministries for them. And it is unfortunate that so much ministry potential in the local church has gone unrealized.

The people in our churches have tremendous ministry potential, but they are often frustrated that the church program has no outlet for that potential. Recently I was in another city and spoke with a young man who came out of the drug culture and a young lady who came out of an incestuous home. Both had a desire to minister to people who are having or in the past have had similar experiences. But their churches' middle-class orientation hasn't produced a place for them to minister.

The most frequent complaint I hear from fellow pastors is that church structure prevents them from getting involved in much meaningful ministry. When local churches were preparing for "Here's Life, Denver" a pastor confided that he was going to leave the pastorate if this campaign didn't have a major impact on his church. He was boxed in by his church's expectations. They expected him to visit the shut-ins weekly. (Many of those "shut-ins" managed to get out for numerous other things, but never for church.) He was expected to be at endless committee meetings since he was an ex officio member of all church committees. Add to these, counseling, hospital visitation, looking after the building and preparing two Sunday sermons, one Wednesday evening message and an adult Sunday School lesson—no wonder he felt trapped. Unfortunately, "Here's Life" did not have much of an impact on his church and he has since left the pastorate.

We have created tremendous ministry problems in the local church by boxing in our lay people and pastors alike. Add to that our preoccupation with the middle class and our narrow range of ministries and it's little wonder the couple's story in the beginning of this chapter is so common. We will have to make a concentrated effort to unleash our churches if we are to break out of our suburban captivity.

*As a result of our middle-class focus, we have become "ministry-poor."* After receiving my early training as a Christian in a parachurch organization, I was amazed to see how "ministry-helpless" most people in the churches are. For example, if you say to someone trained by the Navigators, "There's an apartment complex; let's have a ministry there," he knows what you mean and he knows what to do. He knows that to have a ministry you must find a point of contact. That means possibly moving in and inviting people over for dinner. Or it may mean hanging around the basketball court and getting to know some of the guys by playing ball with them. Once he has earned a hearing, he'll have opportunities to communicate the gospel, not only with his life but also verbally. And if God enables him to lead someone to Christ, he'll start the process of personal follow-up.

On the other hand, if you were to say to the average Baptist or Presbyterian, "There's an apartment complex; let's have a ministry there," he would have no idea what you meant. Because he thinks of ministry as some form of church work. And church work happens inside a church building. Therefore, the church person needs a Sunday School class to teach, a choir to sing in, a committee to serve on. He is too ministry-crippled to see beyond these typical activities.

I do not mean to imply that ministries taking place inside church buildings are wrong. Persons teaching Sunday School or singing in the choir meet the needs of the Body. Their ministries are very important. It's just that they are not enough if we are to fulfill the Great Commission completely.

Several years ago, while pastoring the First Presbyterian Church of Hollywood, Richard Halverson learned what he called a "significant" lesson. He was approached by a leading layman who had been elected president of the local school board. This meant a key layman would have to drop some of his church responsibilities. At first, Pastor Halverson bridled at the thought of losing so active a worker. After more consideration, however, he reached a surprising conclusion. In *How I Changed My Thinking About the Church*, he shares his thoughts: "As I pondered the loss of this fine young man . . . I asked . . . 'How many do we need to really do the work of the organization of this church?' . . . many of the men and women in the church had several jobs. . . . They were very busy with the ecclesiastical establishment. But suppose that each could hold only one job, how many would it take to do the work of that large congregation? At the time, the membership was about 7,000. To my amazement I found that it would require only 365 to do the work that was required to maintain the program of the First Presbyterian Church of Hollywood. . . . This meant that most of the members of the church could never have a job in the institution. It followed . . . that if the work of the church is what is done for the institution, very few, relatively speaking, will ever have an opportunity to do the work of the church."[5]

Halverson wrote these insights over a decade

ago. Still, things have not changed significantly. In a recent survey, Larry Richards and his colleagues asked 5,000 pastors what the greatest needs are for strengthening the church. On a scale of five from a twenty-five-item list, nearly 100 percent gave a first or second priority to "*Getting my lay people involved as ministering men and women.*"

The approach to ministry of most churches, then, is not wrong. It simply is not big enough. It's not big enough to reach this generation which is largely outside the middle-class family unit, nor is it big enough to get the majority of church people involved in ministry. It has, in fact, made our churches ministry-deficient.

*The local church has a lot to learn from parachurch groups.* The church should begin to recognize the parachurch ministries' high ratio of success. By now many of them have had years of experience in areas we in the churches know little about.

When Bear Valley began a serious work with international students, we worked closely with the parachurch organization, International Students, Inc. Their local staff people and national headquarters helped us get started. As the strategic potential of reaching students who will one day be the world's leaders became clearer to us, we added a couple to our staff to specialize with that target group. We have continued to go to International Students, Inc. for help and they have continued their support.

Like International Students, most parachurch organizations want to work with local churches. They want to help unleash the tremendous potential now locked into nearsighted church programs.

Throughout this book I will be pleading with the local church to get involved in ministries which in recent years have been parachurch domains. This should not be understood as a plea for the local church to see itself as the exclusive agency of God's ministry. We need to continue to support and encourage parachurch ministries. The plea is for the local church to get back into the ball game. We have done a fairly good job with the middle class. Let's continue to develop the middle-class ministries God has blessed over the years. But let's also develop a whole new range of ministries, ministries that in the past have been the responsibility of side groups. We're beginning to see that a middle-class-ministries-only mentality is wrong. Not only can we undertake most of the specialized ministries but, because we *are* the church, we have an important advantage. We are the local, visible, functioning Body of Christ. No other organization has the body-dynamic we have.

Collectively, the church is the Body and Bride of Christ, empowered by the Holy Spirit to accomplish God's purposes on earth. Believers are not to see themselves as individuals only, but as necessary, vital members of a Body, which is the church. The local church is the visible manifestation of this Body, ordained by God to carry His witness and to be salt and light to the world. In too many instances we have abrogated this responsibility to a needy world and have turned inward, ministering only to ourselves. We are "the church of the Living God, the pillar and ground of the truth."[6]

## Someday We All Turn Twenty
When I entered seminary I had little knowledge of the local church. I had become a Christian while

serving overseas in the army. For the first seven years of my Christian life, I had served the Lord primarily outside a local church context. During my seminary studies, however, two courses really turned me on to the local church. First, Church History gave me a perspective on where the church has been. As I looked at the church through the ages I saw a tremendous flexibility. The church has been able to function sometimes gloriously, at other times less than gloriously, in virtually every type of culture for 2,000 years.

The second course that gave me a deep appreciation for the church was Systematic Theology. Through studying theology I saw the magnificence of the Body. In light of the Scripture's teaching on the Body, I had to rethink my parachurch experience. Yes, the parachurch is effective because it specializes, but it pays a high price for that effectiveness. The parachurch organization has an intended narrowness built into it. If a ministry is geared for teens, it's great while we're teenagers, but someday we all turn 20. If a ministry is geared for 18-35 year olds, what happens at 36? Perhaps the ministry is geared to street people. What happens when we go straight?

Most parachurch ministries will agree that they are not structured to minister to someone through all the stages of his or her life. Therefore, the constant theme of the parachurch groups is that their objective is to reach certain target groups and to channel them into local churches. But we have had enough history on the recent parachurch explosion to know that these transitions into the local church can be difficult and many never really make it.

The reasons many people who are evangelized and discipled in parachurch ministries don't do well in local churches are varied. But one major reason is the limited scope of ministry in the average local church. People in parachurch ministries are used to doing ministry. But in the local church they are expected to be primarily spectators watching the professionals do the ministry.

One can't help but appreciate the large numbers of people that have been reached and discipled by the various parachurch groups. While we can appreciate their work, we in the local church dare not underestimate our own potential for effective ministry to a wide variety of people.

### The Beauty of the Body

The more I consider God's design for the local church the more amazed I am. The Body is designed to minister to us from bed babies to senior adults. All along the way it has the responsibility and the capacity to nourish us, challenge us, instruct us and build us up in the faith. There is something extremely valuable about a setting where all ages of God's family come together. In 1 Corinthians 12, Paul states at length that the Body needs all of its parts—the weaker, less honorable and unpresentable parts are all necessary. This diversity is hard to find in the highly specialized organization of the parachurch. When it comes to body dynamic, we in the local church have a great advantage.

Practically, however, we have sold ourselves short in our potential to specialize. While the overall beauty of the Body is obvious, we have not paid sufficient attention to the particular parts. The Body has specialized parts capable of ministering to sailors, people in jail, street people, artists, and many others. And they can do these ministries as a *functioning part* of the *local*, visible *church body*. Scripture has left the structure of the local church flexible enough so that we can include special target groups into our ministries.

If we will build specialized ministries into our churches as the parachurch is doing, we will have a great advantage with those we evangelize and disciple. When we in the local church reach that unchurched teenager for Christ we don't have a *transition* problem. We don't have to try to get him into another group because someday he will turn twenty and no longer fit in with us. We are designed to minister to him through all the stages of his life.[7]

## Needed: A Happy Marriage

On the basis of what we have already discussed, I'd like to propose a marriage. As we think about the future of the local church, let's think of a happy marriage between the local church Body and the parachurch target-group ministry. If this marriage is to be a happy one, we cannot abandon our commitment to the middle-class family unit. That means we will continue to recognize the importance of the traditional church ministries. Many within our ranks will be called to major in the ministries of the Sunday School, the choir, auxiliary programs, etc. Others will be called to work with ex-convicts and street people as their *church* ministry. It's not a matter of *superiority*; rather it's a matter of *diversity*. We need not settle for (1) the Christian bypassing the church to reach a target group, or (2) the Christian in the church having opportunities to work only within the fortress; we can have (3) the two working together in a happy marriage. Those working primarily within the home base will be partners with those who use it as a base of operation for outreach to special target groups. If we consider the church in terms of this marriage we will have taken an important step toward the unleashing of the church.

The happy marriage we've been talking about will not be an easy match to arrange. There are several issues we must deal with first. For example, there is a clash in our churches between rural and urban values. One reason the parachurch ministries—born since the late thirties—have been so successful is that they were born in the city. They are in tune with the "urban psyche." They function effectively in the city because that is all they have ever known. The local church, on the other hand, is still tied to its rural past. Therefore, before we can bring together the parachurch target group ministry with the local church body, we need to understand the urban psyche, the rural psyche and their different value systems.

**Notes**

1. *Para* means alongside of; hence, organizations ministering alongside the church.
2. Roy C. Price, "Building Trust Between Pastor and Congregation," *Leadership*, Spring Quarter 1980, p. 50.
3. Stephen Board. "The Great Evangelical Power Shift," *Eternity*, June 1979, p. 17.
4. *Ibid.*
5. Richard C. Halverson, *How I Changed My Thinking About the Church*, (Grand Rapids: Zondervan Publishing House, 1972), pp. 73,74.
6. Richard S. Houtz, "Learning to Be a Family," *Christianity Today*, June 6, 1980, p. 21.
7. See 1 John 2:7,12-14, *New International Version*.

**Chapter 2**

# Are There Farmers in the City Church?

The lecturer was billed as an expert on the city. Approximately twenty-five of us pastors had gathered to hear the author of *How Churches Grow in an Urban World!* Dr. Dubose shared numerous statistics and insights with us. But perhaps his quote from Harvard theologian Harvey Cox summed up best the tone of the conference: "Future historians will record the Twentieth Century as that century in which the whole world became one immense city."[1] Add to that the statement by Roger Greenway, a former missionary to Sri Lanka and Mexico, "The only conclusion we can reach is that at no time in history has it been more true than now that he who wins the city, wins the world"[2]—and we begin to see the importance of city ministries.

Today most people live in cities. In Colorado, for example, sixty percent of the population is in the Denver metropolitan area. This trend toward the city is likely to continue. The next phase will probably be a move from metropolis (mother cities) to megalopolis (the great city). In Colorado that would mean a city on the front range of the Rockies from Fort Collins to Pueblo. In California it would mean solid city from Los Angeles to the Mexican border.

If we Christians are going to be serious about the Great Commission at this moment in history, we must be serious about reaching the cities.

The Scripture has much to say about the city, from the city of Enoch in Genesis to the New Testament city of Jerusalem.[3] Quoting Greenway again: "The Bible contains fourteen hundred references to the city, and there are at least twenty-five examples of what can be called urban ministry in the historical books alone."[4] Modern Christians must look first at Scripture and then at the cultural condition of our cities before designing a strategy to reach urban areas for Christ.

The dominance of cities in America is a recent development. Even fifty years ago most Americans lived in small towns. One-hundred years ago they lived on farms. It is important to understand that it was in that period of the rural dominance of the frontier that America's largest protestant denominations experienced unparalleled growth.

### Looking Back

The two largest protestant denominations in America are the Southern Baptists and the United Methodists. At the time of the American Revolution, however, Methodists were almost nonexistent in America and, numerically, the Baptists ranked behind the Episcopalians, Presbyterians and Congregationalists. One-hundred years later Methodists and Baptists were by far the largest groups. Why?

Obviously there were many reasons, but they can be summed up by saying that these denominations had an effective strategy for reaching the expanding frontier, while others did not. Methodists and Baptists were the modern men of Issachar "who understood the times and knew what Israel [or, in this case, the churches on the frontier] should do."

Prior to the Revolution, the strongest denominations insisted that their churches be pastored by educated men. In practice, this meant trained clergymen. But the frontier was expanding westward at a rapid pace. Settlements were springing up and there were no fresh graduates to send either to start new churches or to pastor those already formed. When hastily built churches were fortunate enough to get a pastor, he often was not suitable for the situation. His eastern education separated him from the people of the frontier. He was prone to speak over their heads about issues which held little interest for them. Since he frequently was the only one who could read or write in the entire town, he might be diverted from his pastoral duties to become the local school teacher. Such problems rendered confirmed denominations nearly incapable of evangelizing rough, uneducated frontiersmen.

These large established denominations were married to the pre-Revolutionary era. During that time Colonial America had become relatively static. Citizens looked to England for their identity. But after the Revolution, a new chapter in the story developed as people surged toward the frontiers. Some historians have contended that American history did not really begin until this frontier period. Only two denominations were able to keep up with the westward movement. Only two groups demonstrated the qualities of Issachar.

*The Methodist circuit rider.* Since the Methodists were almost nonexistent in America before the Revolution, they weren't tied to a period in the past. Nor were they tied to formal educational institutions. Their leadership sprang up from within their "methodical" study groups, called societies. With this lay training, a burning commitment, and the call to preach, the Methodist circuit riders rapidly covered the western territories. They systematically divided up the new territory into circuits. Then they paid the price to carry out the Great Commission. Some of the most courageous and innovative pages of church history come out of this circuit-rider era. One man could pastor several churches even though he couldn't be with them all the time. The circuit riders traversed the entire frontier while the major denominations were able to produce leadership for only a tiny fraction of it.

*The Baptist farmer-preacher.* Baptists approached evangelization of the frontier differently but also with much success. Preachers for Baptist churches often *emerged* out of the community. They were usually uneducated farmers with a call to preach. Their zealous commitment to God communicated to frontiersmen better than the seminary training of the large denomination pastors. Since the Baptist churches in frontier communities produced their own preachers they did not have to wait for one to arrive from the East. In this way they established a firm, grass-roots foothold, while established churches receded farther and farther into the background.

When the dust on the frontier began to settle, the largest protestant denominations were the Methodists and the Baptists. Their growth was a direct result of their evangelizing methods and of their ability to produce pastors from among the people. They adapted successfully to the frontier environment then and they continue to be the largest denominations today. It remains to be seen, however, who will successfully adapt to urban environments of the present and the future.

It is quite ironic that the rural values which fostered success for the Baptists on the frontier may well prove to produce certain failure a hundred years later.

### Rural Values Versus Urban Values

The farm is more than a place; it is a mind-set. The same is true for the city. There is a rural psyche and an urban psyche, definite, distinct attitudes and ways of approaching life. These two mind-sets have different value systems which are often in conflict with each other. Most people either really like a rural area or they really like the city. Not many are indifferent.

The conflict between the rural and urban value systems is, however, not the same kind of conflict that exists between biblical and worldly values. The issue in the latter case is a matter of right and wrong but the issue between rural and urban values is merely one of preference. It is not a matter of which set of values is right or even best.

What is the issue? The issue is a pragmatic one. Rural values work best in rural settings and urban values work best in urban settings. City churches, however, have tried to function in an urban setting while retaining rural values. The evangelical church in the city has become an odd entity; the style of the church's operation is out of joint with urban life, not because it is more holy, but because it is more rural.

Much of the following material on rural and urban values is drawn from the conference on the city mentioned at the beginning of this chapter. Having been raised in a small North Dakota town, and having later lived in Los Angeles and Denver, I had already become aware of these two distinct mind-sets. But Dubose's thoughts on the city helped me to better understand the clash between rural and urban values.

### Status Quo Versus Change

In a rural setting the status quo normally prevails. When I return to my hometown after being away for two or three years, things haven't changed much. My father will point out a new house or two; a business may have folded and a new one opened, but the town remains very much the same, as does the power structure. The same people own the bank, large amounts of land, etc. As you talk to people about the old days they often say, "Ya, things don't change much around here." That's true—they don't.

In the city, however, change is the accepted way of life. If I leave Denver for a month I can see all sorts of changes when I return. Gas stations have become submarine sandwich shops; new neighbors have moved in; housing developments have sprung up where open fields were; new types of businesses have opened. Yesterday I had never heard of a "tanning center." (I assume it's a place where people can buy suntans all year round.) Today there is one near my house. Many businesses open and fold within a few months.

Perhaps the power structure remains basically the same in that it is controlled by the moneyed few, but millionaires are declaring bankruptcy and others taking their place in a constantly changing pattern. In the city one lives with change.

Likewise, the city church must learn to live with change. Of course our message is unchanging: Jesus is the same yesterday, today and forever. But our methods of ministry must stay flexible, capable of changing.

Culture does not stay the same. In the city it changes more rapidly than in the rural area. The needs and opportunities for ministry are also constantly changing. At one time we had a group of fifty to sixty Laotians worshiping with us in one of our congregations. Since then they have formed their own church and the worship service, of which they had been a part, is quite different without them. We once had a Saturday evening worship service. We no longer have one, but may start one again in the future. If our people could not live with change, much of our ministry would be severely hindered.

We evangelicals cannot afford to allow our churches to become the bastions of the status quo. When we have the opportunity to enhance the ministry of the gospel by changing, we must be prepared to change and, when called for, we must change quickly.

Most of the people in our churches consider change a normal part of their lives. Yesterday McDonald's sold only hamburgers and fish; today you can eat breakfast there! In their vocations our people have been taught to think, How can we improve, expand our markets, do a better job? Yet, they have not been taught to think in these terms about the church. When they relate to the church and its ministries they shift from the city value of change to the rural value of maintaining the status quo. We church people embrace two value systems: one we apply to our work, our business, our "real" world and the other value system we apply to our church.

## Sameness Versus Diversity

Rural areas are oriented not only toward the status quo, but also toward sameness. Admittedly, the difference here is a fine one. Maintaining the status quo was set against change, while sameness is set against diversity. What is in view here is an insistence on living a similar life-style, on being like one's friends. It would be difficult for a black family to live comfortably in most small all-white towns and vice versa. The average small town in the North wouldn't accept the building of a Buddhist temple as readily as it would a Lutheran church.

To illustrate further, recently my wife and I took a tour of San Francisco. Our driver took us through a large homosexual section of the city and gave us some information on the "gay culture." Most small towns would not be likely to tolerate even one homosexual, let alone a whole homosexual subculture.

To say that the church must appreciate the diversity of the city is not to say we must approve of homosexuality or other sinful practices, but we must recognize their presence. They are in the city in large numbers and our Lord loves those who practice such things as much as He loves any other sinner. Therefore, the city church should become diverse enough in its outreach to minister to them.

We simply cannot have an Archie Bunker mentality toward those who are different. Granted, Archie Bunker is an urbanite. The intention here is not to say prejudice is only a small-town phenomenon. Unfortunately, prejudice is alive and well in the urban as well as the rural areas. That's what makes Archie's life a series of interesting stories. Because he is in the city he must deal with black neighbors, Jewish shopkeepers, an atheist son-in-law, an oriental pastor, etc. It is his insistence on sameness in the midst of tremendous urban diversity that makes the show a success. A stubborn refusal to accept the realities of life in the big city may be a great story line for a situation comedy, but it is a self-defeating mind-set for effective ministry in the city.

Over and against sameness is the urban value of diversity. When pollsters attempt to find out which city Americans desire most to live in, San Francisco often comes out on top. One of the main reasons given for any city's popularity is its diversity. The city presents unending variables and city people like that. If a church is to have an effective urban ministry it must understand and accept this diversity of the city.

The fortress church does not accept the principle of diversity. It offers a limited number of ministries. If a lay person doesn't fit into the narrow range of these half dozen or so ministries, he or she has nothing to do in the church. Some people in our churches would be effective in ministering to recent immigrants and there are plenty of them in our cities. But the church is not structured to reach this group. The same is true for street people, unwed mothers and the unchurched elderly. Still others have a special calling to minister to homosexuals. The evangelical church should be providing a framework within which Christians can minister to these diverse groups which comprise the city.

Recognizing and ministering to all the elements of the city is a key to unleashing the church. But we must come to grips with the diversity within the city church as well as the diversity of the community. If a church has a street ministry, a girls' home and a refugee ministry, it can anticipate some of these people coming to its worship services.

What can we do to accommodate the diverse elements who come together to worship? We still have much to learn in this area at Bear Valley but we have discovered a helpful approach. We have structured two completely different types of worship services. One, a traditional service, has a choir, an order of worship, etc. It adopts the form most people would expect when visiting a Baptist church. We also have what is called, for lack of a better name, an "alternate" service. This congregation meets in the Fellowship Hall with chairs in an informal circle. They share Scripture and prayer requests, take a coffee break during which the sharing becomes one-to-one, and worship together through singing and hearing the Word preached. The sermon, however, is the same one given in the traditional service.

There are those who need and appreciate the order of a formal worship service. Others, however, are spiritually enriched by worshiping in the more spontaneous atmosphere of one of the alternate congregations. We can be flexible and creative in our approach to worship—diversity is not a sin. We do not have to strictly adhere to one form of worship and compel everyone else to do the same.

The slowness of the church to respond to the diversity inherent in the Great Commission is nothing new. As we read the book of Acts we see an agonizing struggle over the issue of diversity. To the amazement of the narrow-minded believers

God allowed Samaritans (those half-breed, heretical black sheep of the Jewish race in Jerusalem) to respond to the gospel. He even gave them the same Pentecostal gifts He had earlier given to the Jewish church. And then came the most radical command of all. In Acts 10, God compelled Peter to minister to full-blooded Gentiles in the home of Cornelius. What was the church coming to?

The church was simply coming to a state of obedience. Jesus gave the Jewish church the Great Commission to go into all the world and make disciples of every nation. But what Jesus said and what they heard were two different things. They heard a mandate to preach the gospel to Jews everywhere. Similarly today, the American church has heard the mandate to take the gospel to the American middle class and to unchristianized cultures overseas. We have not usually understood that the Great Commission includes as well the diverse subcultures so prevalent in America.

The acceptance of differing ethnic backgrounds and life-styles did not come easily to the New Testament church. We should not expect it to be easy for us. However, in the midst of dissimilar city cultures, we should find within the local church a tolerance and an appreciation of diversity.

## Harmony Versus Conflict-Management

We have seen that rural America is more likely to value the status quo and sameness while the city tends to value change and diversity. Rural areas are also more likely to insist on harmony over conflicting elements.

For example, the town in which I grew up has a history of liberal theology dominating the most influential churches. Their memberships rarely heard the message conveying the need to be "born again." But once when I was a boy a young preacher came to one of those churches. His preaching was zealously evangelistic—unusual for that church. In fact, he boldly tried to compete with the town's chief amusement on those long, summer Saturday nights. He set up his microphone across the street from two of the busiest bars in the town and sent the population into an uproar, because in a North Dakota farming community Saturday night is for heavy drinking and partying. And of course you don't preach at people (many of whom were church members) trying to party at the local bars on Saturday evening and then calmly meet them in church on Sunday.

It wasn't long before that preacher moved on. Many of us can appreciate his boldness and admit we do not know how the Lord was leading him. From a human point of view he probably would have had a much longer and more effective ministry if he had not caused so much conflict. (Perhaps it would have served him well to study the culture he was entering.)

But in an urban setting, street preachers come and go without much notice. City people realize there is no single, well-defined social order. The city is a melting pot containing more than one set of values, more than one culture; it is the place where values and cultures merge. Therefore, in the city we have no illusions about eliminating conflict. The street preacher may irritate us but we are not likely to be able to get rid of him. In the city we must learn to manage the conflict.

At Bear Valley one of our congregations is more of a melting pot than the others. It is made up of middle-class family units, many singles, street people and some antiestablishment thinkers.

There are points of tension in this service. For example, the middle-class people like to sing from a hymnal accompanied by a piano. The street people prefer passages of Scripture set to music with guitars or maybe a banjo. We'll probably never have harmony on this issue; we have to settle for *conflict-management.*

Through trial and error we have found an approach which seems to work. We simply split up. Half the time a middle-class person leads the music and half the time a street person leads. Each group, in time, learns to appreciate the other. It has been good for street people to establish friendships with middle-class people and vice versa. In fact, many in this congregation are attracted to it because of this very quality of diversity. We don't believe we ought to force people to relate to others in different subcultures. But we feel it's a healthy thing for the whole church when the opportunity to do so exists.

In the city church then, we must learn to live with conflict. It must not deter us from ministering in obedience to Christ's commands. Over a year ago our church obtained a license from the state of Colorado to operate a girls' home. The possibilities of conflict in this ministry were enormous. There were possible clashes with the state and counties, as well as contention within the staff because of the intense nature of their work. We were licensed for ten girls, and the conflict which ten girls with major problems might generate seemed almost unlimited.

The ministry did indeed promise and deliver a lot of conflict. But it was a strategic ministry. The home became a contact point with girls who were wards of the state. We did not cram Christianity down their throats. But we did give them the opportunity to live in a group home staffed by Christians, who modeled Christlikeness in their day-to-day living.

After nearly a year of operation, two girls have made public commitments to Christ and have experienced public baptism. Others have privately committed their lives to Christ. This type of home represents a portion of the city the church has nearly abandoned. It is filled with both conflict and tremendous opportunities for ministry. To carry on this ministry we cannot anticipate continual harmony; we are much wiser if we learn *conflict-management.*

## Smallness Versus Bigness

Upon returning to my boyhood town as an adult the overwhelming impression was, "I can't believe how small it is." I can jog from one edge of town to the other in about ten minutes. When I talk to people in my hometown about Denver they often say, "Yes, I'll bet it's a nice place but I wouldn't want to live there; it's too big."

People often live in the country or in small towns because they value smallness. To many of these people bigness is threatening. They feel they lose control as things become bigger. They do not like the feeling of anonymity and insignificance which big cities breed. I recall my mother's answer when I asked her why they stayed in such a small town for so many years. Without a hint of criticism she replied, "Your father enjoys being a big fish in a small pond." As the pond gets bigger, the fish seem smaller.

The city, on the other hand, is geared toward bigness. Big buildings, big car dealers, big supermarkets, big shopping centers are the norm. If you want to see a professional sports contest you had better be prepared for a big crowd. The city *is* big and the city *thinks* big.

When a church thinks small in the city it is out of pace with its environmental psyche. We must, of course, carefully guard against following or acceding to the prevailing culture in those areas which are contrary to Scripture. The church, however, can maintain its testimony of calling the world to repentance while at the same time adjusting to the demands and challenges of the environment around it, even the environment of a city.

People are conditioned to think big in the city. Big is not necessarily bad; in fact, it can be very good. I like what Elton Trueblood said: "Whatever else our Lord had in mind, it is clear that He envisioned something very big. He did not propose a slight change in an existing religion! The radical nature of the proposed church is indicated by the fact that in one chapter of the New Testament, Christ is reported three times as saying, 'Something greater is here' (Matthew 12:6,41,42)."[5]

We must have big churches in the city because the city is big. Big churches, however, do not necessarily mean big buildings with huge parking lots. The types of buildings will come up again in chapter 8. At the moment we are talking about big churches and not big church buildings. We cannot afford to keep our churches small so that we can be big fish in a small pond. We cannot afford to be afraid of losing control. The size of the modern city demands that we think big.

### Established Versus Mobile

Perhaps this last set of values is not as central as those we have already discussed, but it is important. In a rural setting, life is fairly stationary. Everything is nearby. Occasionally it becomes necessary to travel to the nearest city to get certain items but daily needs are readily available close to home. One does not expect to travel extensively or often except under special circumstances.

In the city, mobility is a way of life. I drive a few miles to work, a few more to the library, across town to a distant hospital, then make a house call and the round trip totals twenty-five miles. Later, perhaps, I will attend a meeting in another distant part of the city.

City people are mobile. In most gatherings of city people someone has just returned from Chicago or Los Angeles while someone else is planning to leave for Atlanta or New York City. A stewardess in our singles group, for instance, works out of Kansas City but lives in Denver.

Many are predicting this mobility will change because of the energy shortage. I would not advise planning neighborhood churches just yet. In the city, people will still have to travel because that is the way cities have been constructed. Chances are good that we will always find ways to stay mobile. Improved public transportation, electric cars or something else will keep us moving.

In the past it has been a mistake to think in terms of the neighborhood church in the city and it will continue to be a mistake. Most cities are not neighborhood conscious. (Exceptions are some of the ethnic communities of big eastern cities. They may be even more stable than rural communities since they are usually united in more facets of life: religion, politics, customs, race and even language.) Most people will remain city-conscious as opposed to neighborhood-conscious. They will continue in the future to pass several churches to get to the one they want to attend. City people are used to traveling, and mobility is a way of life.

## City Churches Need Leaders Who Think as City People

The urban church that is in tune with its environment will be accustomed to change, diversity, conflict-management, bigness and mobility. It is not strange that much of the lay leadership in city churches think in terms of city values in their professional worlds. But for some reason these same leaders seek to maintain the rural values of status quo, sameness, harmony, smallness and inertia in their churches. Or perhaps they really do not want these rural values in the church, but because such values have been in the church for so long, many lay people think they must somehow be scriptural.

Toward the conclusion of Dr. Dubose's seminar on the city I sensed a tremendous amount of frustration on the part of the pastors present. With his help, most were able to see that city pastors are being asked to lead institutions that are in urban settings but dominated by rural values. For the great majority, it is not working. Their churches are not growing and they are experiencing a continual turnover of pastoral leadership. But still they continue to try to pump life into the same old dead programs. It is a losing proposition to be asked to function in the city with lay or vocational leadership that wants the church to be the last bastion of rural values.

Dr. Dubose greatly encouraged me to continue in the direction of expanding the vision of our church to meet the challenge of the city. I felt reaffirmed in my conviction that God has led Bear Valley to a commitment to principles that are scriptural and at the same time in tune with an urban setting.

Once we understand the issues surrounding the urban and rural psyches, we need to get a grasp on target-grouping the city. If we no longer see the city primarily as middle-class family units we need to ask ourselves, Who else is there? Once we discover the answer to that question, the urban mind-set which understands change, diversity, conflict-management, bigness and mobility will spur us into reaching the cities' target groups.

### Notes

1. Quoted by Dr. Dubose in a lecture entitled, "How Churches Grow in an Urban World."
2. Roger S. Greenway, *Apostles to the City* (Grand Rapids: Baker Book House, 1978), p. 11.
3. See Genesis 4:17; Revelation 21:2.
4. Greenway, *Apostles to the City*, p. 11.
5. Elton Trueblood, *The Incendiary Fellowship* (New York: Harper and Row Publishers, 1967), p. 100.

# Chapter 3

# Target-Grouping the City

As the street worker was about to board the van to return to the Genesis Center—a communal home for Christian street people—he noticed a young girl holding a basket standing nearby. Though he had already been on the street witnessing for several hours he decided he should talk to just one more person. During the conversation he discovered she didn't have a place to stay so he invited her to join them at the Genesis Center. After sizing up the situation for a moment, she agreed and boarded the van. The sound of crying from the basket made it obvious that she was carrying a baby.

The street worker mentioned above is not a member of Teen Challenge or some other parachurch ministry. He is a church member who specializes in ministry to street people. His base of operations is the Genesis Center, a communal home where fifteen to thirty people live. It is part of Bear Valley, a local church ministry.

The young mother mentioned represents one of many target groups—the street people. Hundreds of people in the city simply live on the street, just drifting from one place to another. As we think of this young mother we have to ask, How would she have fed herself and her baby that evening? She was broke and she didn't know anyone in Denver. Some people in her situation would have ended up in a city or privately supported welfare center of some sort. Most, however, would try to cope for themselves on the street. For young women, that usually means prostitution, nude modeling, etc., because they think they have no other choices.

Where are most of the churches in relationship to the street culture? In a word—nowhere. Most simply don't have the contact point to reach street people for Christ. We can be sure that "business as usual" programs will never enable us to make that contact. If we want to have an effective ministry to street people we must learn to target-group them.

## What Is a Target Group?

I have been using the term *target group* and I need to explain more fully what I mean. When a sociologist looks at cultures he or she looks at the groupings within the culture. Hence, in sociology we study about nuclear families, extended families, peer groups, white- and blue-collar workers, upper, middle and lower classes, ethnic groups, etc.

Seeing the city as a collection of target groups is seeing the city as a Christian sociologist sees it. We look for groupings of people and design ministries with their life-styles in mind. We already have children ministries and youth ministries in our churches. It shouldn't be difficult to see the possibilities of street ministries and cult ministries.

Then add perhaps less obvious groups such as artists and writers. (Our church now ministers to
both of these.) And certainly musicians present
yet another possibility. A professional musician
recently joined our church. He knows dozens of
other musicians in the city, but only one other
who is a Christian. He feels isolated from the
Christian community. This man and others like
him work unusual hours. Their life-styles are
often quite different from those of the middle
class. They are not likely to be drawn to a setting
that is geared for the average suburban family.
They need something designed for them. They are
a target group.

Once we become aware of a target group, we
must then ask, How do we make contact with it? If
we fail to see these sociological groupings in the
city and fail to make contact with them, God will
probably call other specialized parachurch ministries to do the job. Target groups abound and they
increasingly claim larger percentages of the total
population. In the church our choice is to either
target-group the city and get back in touch with
the other two-thirds of the people, or carry on
business as usual with the shrinking middle
class.

Since the local church has structured itself out
of contact with nearly everyone except the middle
class, it has had to depend on the parachurch to
form arms for the local bodies. How many times
have we heard parachurch representatives report
on their ministry and ask for prayer and financial
support? When doing so they will inevitably
explain that they are but an arm of the local
church. This method does have its place but it
becomes ridiculous when hundreds of outsiders
dash in for support, then dash out to some excit-

ing front-line ministry, leaving the church to baby-sit the middle class. This is not the fault of the dasher, but of the church which somehow has become conditioned to think it can only pray and give monetary aid if the ministry is beyond its usual programs.

While in seminary we future pastors had visions of serving the radiant bride of Christ. Yet when we were called to serve a local church we found something that resembled a shriveled octopus more than a bride with a beautiful body. Our bride didn't have her own arms. Others had stuck their arms all over her. Her ministry activity was so small she had shrunk to a few programs, scores of committees and maintenance of a building or two.

We went to our pulpits, opened our Bibles and preached, "The Lord's message rang out from you not only in Macedonia and Achaia—your faith in God has become known everywhere" (1 Thess. 1:8). But our preaching had a hollow ring. Words like "everywhere" stuck in our throats as we looked over congregations that had very little involvement or even contact with large segments of our community. We knew that the distance between the church spoken of in the Bible and the one we were serving was immense.

The distance doesn't have to be that great. The "everywhere" can become a reality. We can go everywhere in the city as the church, the Bride of Christ. As God leads us, equips us, and gives us the vision, we can go. I am not advocating competing with parachurch organizations nor withdrawing our support of them. Rather, let's join hands with them and reenter fields we have abandoned. The target groups of the city are too large to quibble over who is going to minister to them. For every young woman like the one mentioned earlier there are a hundred others whose needs are as great. It's true, parachurch organizations are equipping thousands for effective target-group ministries. In spite of that, local churches still have the vast manpower potential for reaching this generation for Christ. To accomplish that task we need to consider what is involved in target-grouping the city.

## Step One—Seeing the Invisible

The first step in target-grouping is learning to see what has been invisible. One of our Lord's constant frustrations was that His followers did not see what He saw. All they saw in Zacchaeus was a despicable little tax collector. But Jesus saw someone who needed a friend and, more than that, someone who needed deliverance from his sin.

At Jacob's well one day, Jesus' followers saw only a Samaritan woman who looked as though she had been through the mill. But He saw a precious, hurting human being who could be the key to spreading the gospel in Samaria. Over and over again He saw what was invisible to those around Him.

Not long ago we had a young man join our street team who was a "delivered homosexual." He felt called of God to return to the homosexual bars and share his faith and deliverance. One or two nights a week he went to these bars while his wife visited lesbian bars to witness. When we shared this ministry with the church, some remarked that they didn't even know there were such things as homosexual bars in Denver. Such places are simply not visible to our middle-class world.

A major task for the local church body then is to help one another see hitherto invisible segments of our society. Thousands of refugees, for example, can melt into a major city and hardly be noticed. Even though they still receive mention occasionally in the media, most people, including those in our churches, scarcely know they exist.

We need to condition ourselves to see what Jesus saw. It doesn't come naturally, even for the believer. We need to ask ourselves as we move about the city, Who are these people? What is their contact point with the gospel? Is there something God would have me do?

One possible means of making ourselves aware of the needs of the city is to take "seeing-as-He-saw" field trips. For example, go sit in the emergency room of the publicly financed hospital in your community, preferably between 11:00 P.M. and 5:00 A.M. Watch as people come in with gunshot wounds, knife wounds, drug overdoses or battered bodies. Listen as they grope to give their addresses or the name of their next of kin. Sometimes they don't even know their own names. Then, remember that their names are a part of the "whosoever" in John 3:16.

Not all the invisible target groups are outside the middle class. As we condition ourselves to see the city as target groups, we must look at the whole city. We may be surprised to find some target groups right under our noses. Such is the case with MOPS (Mothers of Pre-Schoolers). A couple of years ago a young mother shared with me that her former church had begun a special ministry to mothers with preschool children. She helped me see a target group that had been invisible to me, an extremely important one.

Unless one has experienced it, one cannot fathom what it is like to be cooped up all day with one preschooler, let alone with two or more. These mothers of preschoolers receive very few strokes from a society that is geared to the "working" woman, as though these mothers don't do the toughest work of all. In fact, they probably have the most important role in the entire society. Psychologists keep telling us that the early years are the most important in a child's development. The mother is the first significant other in a child's life, and as such has a huge influence on that child throughout his life. In short, mothers of preschoolers probably have the most strategic role in our culture.

What can we do to minister to these moms? We can bring in specialists to help them be more effective mothers. These specialists can inform our moms of effective communication with preschoolers, physiological development and creative toys. In other words, they can help moms understand what it's like to be a preschooler.

We can also help these young women to form a support group with other mothers. Again we can speak to the spiritual dimension of parenthood. (Recently the Princeton Religion Research Center studied the unchurched and found that seventy-four percent of them want their children to receive religious training.) We can provide a nursery so the moms can have time away from their little ones. (Our nursery stays open on MOPS meeting days into the afternoon so the mothers are free to go out for lunch or do other things they like to do.) There is much we can do to minister to these important people.

And now after two years of target group ministry to MOPS we are beginning to think of more possibilities. What if the Lord were to give us the leadership and show us how to target-group a crowded apartment complex loaded with children? In many of these complexes the anger and despair of the tenants is obvious. Living in such close quarters, many of these people feel trapped as the possibility of ever owning their own homes becomes more remote. So often they vent their frustrations on their innocent, small children. I believe MOPS ministries in apartment buildings could reduce child abuse significantly. In addition, it could give us a contact point with those presently out of touch.

The MOPS target group is a ministry within the middle-class family unit. There are other middle-class target groups that don't fit into the family unit category. Singles and senior citizens would be two such groups. As we look for target groups in the city we need to see the people on the other side of town, but we must also open our eyes to those needs that are close to home as well.

### Step Two—The Holy Spirit's Call to Ministry

Once we see the target group we must then wait for the Holy Spirit to lead someone into that ministry. In John 17 Jesus says, "I have brought you glory on earth by completing the work you gave me to do" (v. 4). Not every blind person had been healed or every tax collector redeemed, but our Lord's work was finished. Not every need constitutes a call to our church. The Lord can be trusted to lead us into the ministries He desires for us.

If a church sees a possible target group but no one is led to minister to it, we must learn to wait with "relaxed concern." On the other hand, lay people often see target groups the pastoral leadership doesn't see. When someone shares that he feels called of the Holy Spirit to begin a ministry to a certain group, pastors and the church as a whole should listen seriously.

Once we are confident that God has enabled us to see the target group and has supplied someone to minister to it, we're ready to begin the ministry. We can now proceed with confidence in two critical areas. First, we're moving into an area where God wants us. Second, our leadership has God-given motivation. We don't want to have to be continually pumping these ministries up. We don't want them based on guilt or someone-ought-to motivation. If they are they will be a drain on the church. Unleashing the church and the critical factor of want-to motivation will be discussed in a later chapter. At this point, I need only mention that want-to motivation is critical before attempting a new target-group ministry.

### Step Three—Learning from the Parachurch Ministries

If God calls the church to minister to a target group, chances are good that some parachurch ministry will already be working in the same field. Target-grouping is a familiar concept to those in parachurch ministries. Most of their organizations exist to carry on specialized ministries to some particular segment of the city. They are accustomed to thinking in terms of going after people.

For most of the churches, however, target-grouping is a new venture. When one speaks about target-grouping in the local church he is likely to be greeted with a blank stare. "Why do we have to design a special ministry for that group? Why can't they attend our regular services like everyone else?" Why? Because they won't. In the church we have developed a fortress mentality which says, "We'll minister to anyone who will come and fit in with us." The parachurch has developed an unleashed mentality which says, "We'll design ministries to go after those who won't come to us."

Therefore, our models for target-grouping come mainly from the parachurch ministries. If we aim for foreign students, for instance, we should ask ourselves, "How does International Students, Inc. minister to foreign students?" Or with street people, "What are some of the things Teen Challenge has found successful in working with them?" Of course, not all the models will be 100 percent positive. We may see things in the parachurch ministries that we will want to do differently.

Beyond the how-to's it is important to look at the attitudes of parachurch organizations toward their staff people. For example, the Navigators spend a lot of time equipping new staff for ministry, but once that person has gained the organization's confidence and is assigned to the field he is given a great degree of freedom. He is expected to remain faithful to his calling and to get the job done. He may use his house as a base or he may not; perhaps he will plan evangelistic rallies, perhaps not. He decides whether it is best to contact students on or off campus. He is not burdened with committees or a fortress mentality that expects him to use the church building as a base of operation. He is free to perform his ministry the way he feels it ought to be done. Yes, he has counsel and help but he is expected to plan and carry out his ministry in the way that is most effective for his particular target group.

We need to look at those who are already ministering to the target groups we're interested in. We need to look at the mechanics, at the attitudes toward staff and the kind of staff they are using.

As we consider the kind of staff the parachurch ministries are using, we need to think about the possibility of adding some new staff positions in our churches. The church unleashed will have to look primarily to its laity to do the work of the ministry. The ministry of the laity, however, is often greatly enhanced when a staff person is working closely with them.

We don't want to get trapped by a status quo attitude toward the church staff. Depending on the size of the church, we might expect to find a pastor, an associate pastor, a nursery coordinator, a Christian education director, music director, and a youth pastor. But what about adding a street pastor, a refugee pastor or a pastor working exclusively with international students? Many churches will want to develop target-group ministries with only lay leadership but we should not automatically eliminate additional vocational staff.

There need not be any conflict between developing laity and hiring more church staff. If the staff understands that they are to assist the lay person in the development of his or her ministry, the vocational staff will enhance a ministering laity.

### Step Four—Becoming Specialists

The fourth step is to carefully study the target group, then devise a strategy to reach it for Christ. Questions need to be answered: How numerous is the target group? What kinds of needs does it have? Most ministries will be built around discovering needs and meeting them. Refugees need someone to teach them English; singles need social activities with other singles; international students need someone to help interpret the culture for them. Everyone needs to hear and understand the gospel and to be given foundational help in their new Christian lives.

A word of caution at this point. We don't need to wait until we have everything figured out before we begin a ministry. We don't need to kill a ministry by assigning a committee to study it. Let's start the ministry! Let's risk making mistakes and learn in the process of ministering.

We knew very little about refugees when we began to minister to them. Now we know much more. We understand some of the racial tension between the Hmong and the Lao, both coming from Laos. We know that the most effective missionary work overseas was done among the Hmong. But they are also low on the cultural totem pole. We have not met any Christians from Cambodia. Very few of them know any English at all. Working with Cambodians has been more difficult than working with the Hmong. Then there are the ethnic Chinese who have played a role in Indochinese commerce similar to that of the Jew in the West. So again we encounter a deeply engrained prejudice.

The people we have working with refugees are serious about understanding their target group. The parachurch organizations have been developing these kinds of specialists for years. Why can't the church? We ought to be grateful for our church specialists in children's work and music. But how about specialists on refugees and ex-convicts? Discovering new target groups and becoming specialists in ministering to them is possible in the local church.

### Step Five—Home Base Can Be Anywhere
The fifth step in target-grouping involves a

change in the way a church views itself and its buildings. The topic of facilities will be developed in a separate chapter. At this point it is only important to mention that to target-group we must think of a ministry beyond that which we are capable of handling in our church buildings. At present, Bear Valley has major ministries based in five locations besides our church address. In the future, these five are likely to grow to many more.

When we consider target-grouping the city we need to see the group first. Then we need to trust the Holy Spirit to lead someone in the church to minister to the group if He wants it done. We can be confident that when He leads someone into a particular ministry, He will supply the internal want-to motivation. If possible we then want to learn as much as we can from others doing this type of ministry. We want to become specialists in this area. That means we never stop learning and improving our techniques. The base operation may be a home, a restaurant, an American Legion Hall, or a church building. If God has led us into the ministry He can be trusted to supply the facilities and finances.

## An Exciting Venture

When a church learns to think in terms of target groups it is in for an exciting adventure. God will raise up people of His choice to minister to various segments in the city. He is not partial to degrees or status or seniority. Throughout our church there is a growing awareness that "God may use me to lead out into a new area of ministry." When a new ministry team is forming, anyone who wants to and feels a leading of the Holy Spirit is welcome to investigate the possibility of participating in that work. Through target-grouping, the Body shapes itself under the leading of the Holy Spirit. We never know what ministry may close or what new ministry the Lord will lead us into. We do, however, know that as long as the Great Commission is still on His heart He will share with His people the burden of taking the gospel everywhere.

In the first chapter we considered a happy marriage between parachurch target-grouping and the local church body-dynamic. We've looked at some of the issues involved, such as the need for an urban mind-set and a willingness to target-group the city.

In the next chapter I want to return to the men of Issachar once again. They understood their times. To understand our times is to know that our cities are desperately in need of aggressive evangelical churches. The large segments of the city where we are not present need us more than ever before.

## Chapter 4

# Believe It or Not, They Need Us

Dr. Vernon Grounds, the former president of a major western seminary, said recently in an interview, "I do think we're witnessing an evangelical renaissance which is astonishing in its proportion. In my college days evangelicals were a tiny minority, viewed as a cultural hangover. By contrast, evangelicalism today is a powerful force in American society."[1] While Dr. Grounds was not all positive in his assessment of the evangelical community, he did affirm that we no longer are seen as a quaint anachronism by our society. Rather, we have become a force to be reckoned with.

Evangelicals are coming out of an era that was shaped by the modernist-fundamentalist controversy in the early twentieth century. Many church historians believe that each side came away from that debate with only half the gospel. The fundamentalist held onto the half that saves the soul; the modernists held on to the half that ministers to the body. But today's evangelicals are trying to put the pieces back together, to proclaim again a whole and living gospel. If they thought it was an either/or option, evangelicals would side with the fundamentalists in a moment. Many, however, are convinced that this is not the case. In fact, a common theme among evangelicals has become, "We must minister to the whole person if we are to minister the whole gospel." More and more people in Bible-believing churches are becoming uncomfortable with merely "saving the soul."

The shift toward a ministry to the whole person has produced some new directions among evangelicals. In Denver, for example, a parachurch organization called Evangelical Concern is coordinating the work of some evangelicals in several areas of social concern. I hasten to point out here that social concern must not be equated with the old "social gospel." Social concern is a legitimate part of the biblical gospel. As Jerry Falwell, a well-known fundamentalist TV preacher, said not long ago in an interview, "I was recently in Thailand refugee camps working with Food for the Hungry, buying food and distributing Bibles . . . you know, there was a day when fundamentalists thought all of that was a waste of time."[2] We have begun to see that ministering to people's physical and emotional needs, as well as their spiritual needs, is not a waste of time. We're right to have moved in this direction. In a country that has so many hurting people we evangelicals are a precious commodity. Since we are so valuable it is imperative that we shift our posture from a defensive stance to an aggressive, offensive position.

### The Fortress Mentality and the Inferiority Complex

The Bible-believing church in America has

been on the defensive too long. When J. Gresham Machen and others left Princeton to form Westminster Seminary in 1929 it appeared to many as a retreat to a new fortress. After the Scopes "monkey" trial in 1925 many felt that a faith based on the authority of Scripture had been made the focus of national ridicule and they busily built more barriers to fend off the liberal attackers.

The defensive posture of those opposing the modernist movement can even be seen in the motto of the Conservative Baptist Theological Seminary in Denver, ". . . [knowing that I am] set for the defense of the gospel."[3] When this school was established, defending the gospel was its primary concern. The Conservative Baptist movement had left the more liberal American Baptist Convention as a result of modernist-fundamentalist controversy. In recent years, however, people connected with the school have wondered aloud if it isn't time to select a new verse. They believe that the motto of the school should be less defensive.

Whether we consider ourselves fundamentalists or evangelicals, we are heir to a mentality that is basically defensive. In fact, it's not too strong to say that we have retreated to our fortresses with a disabling, deep-seated inferiority complex. Subtly the message has come through that the world out there is modern while we are old-fashioned. The world is seen as moving too quickly; it's too affluent, too educated, too sophisticated to be interested in biblical Christianity. In effect, we are ashamed of the gospel of Jesus Christ. We do not believe that the world could possibly want or need what we have.

Today many are trying to change this evangelical posture of retreat from the world. Like those questioning the appropriateness of the seminary motto, many are questioning the fortress mentality and the inferiority complex.

Presently the parachurch ministries are still leading the foray from the fortress back into the American mainstream. Around the country Child Evangelism ministers to unchurched children in backyard clubs. Campus Crusade confronts students on secular campuses and Young Life reaches hard-to-reach teenagers in public high schools with the claims of Christ. (Recently Young Life meetings packed our small fellowship hall with over 200 kids, mostly unchurched.) The Charles Colson prison ministries touch perhaps the most difficult group in all society—the criminal segment.

Not only parachurch groups are ministering to the society at large. Big, successful churches with huge facilities, schools, and television ministries often creatively and aggressively minister outside the fortress.

The problem is the average church with average facilities. This is the segment of the evangelical world which still seems to remain captive to the fortress-mentality/inferiority complex. And it's still the average size church, 100 to 400 people, that has the biggest manpower potential in the evangelical community. For every large successful church in the city there are dozens of small churches that seem to be standing still. By that I mean their impact on the city seems to remain the same year after year.

This average local church with its modest facilities needs to get the message loud and clear: "Believe it or not, they really do need us out there."

Any Bible-believing church can have an effective ministry in the city. There is no reason why any church, under the authority of the Scripture, even with very modest facilities, cannot become the home base for a big ministry. First, however, such churches must be convinced that it really can be done. It can be done without new facilities, without moving to the suburbs and without going on TV. These churches possess the nation's greatest, most precious resource. It's not oil or coal; it's people who still live by a value system based on scriptural absolutes. Every Bible-believing church has the rapidly diminishing commodity of people who love, who can be trusted and who have a common commitment to God's revealed absolutes.

### Taking a Closer Look at This Affluent, Self-Reliant Generation

During the past school year, my oldest daughter was assigned a "me" speech in her psychology class. As the title implies, the students were to tell the class all about themselves. Tami discovered that she was somewhat of an oddball. She was one of only four students out of twenty-eight who still lived with her original parents. This revelation did not come out of a ghetto school, but from a school in a typical middle-class neighborhood.

What used to be thought of as the inner city's problem has now become everyone's problem. Divorce, drugs, alcoholism, loose sex, etc., are now common in suburbia. They have moved next door.

What has happened? Where have our traditional values gone? We are feeling the full impact of those philosophical movements, since the "Enlightenment," that have led us away from biblical revelation. (More reading on this subject is available in the writings of Francis Schaeffer who has traced these movements in detail.) The practical result of this philosophy is a relative ethic based on a fragile secular humanism—the secular humanism which has dominated our educational institutions for the past few decades and has left us with a values vacuum.

*Helping people in a values vacuum.* God has designed us to live in accord with the values revealed in Scripture. These values include certain absolutes. It has been said that we don't break God's laws; they break us. When a society believes that lying, stealing, getting high, having sex outside of marriage, etc. can be okay depending on the circumstances, each person becomes his own god. Each one then devises his or her own guidelines for morality. The situational ethicist looks to "winning through intimidation," "looking out for number one," or any number of dozens of humanist guidelines for ethics. In the end, however, it always reduces to a fallen human being doing what is right in his own eyes. Inevitably that is bad for ourselves and other people.

The result of these anti-Christian philosophies is a treacherous world without an anchor. People are asking, "Is there anyone I can trust; is there anyone who cares?" When we began our ministry to singles in a local restaurant, there were but a handful of single adults in our church. The room in which they began to meet held about 100 people and in only a short time the room was near capacity. The constant theme we heard over and over was how glad they were to find an alternative to the "singles scene." The "singles scene" is one of swinging apartment complexes, discos, singles trips, and an endless search for significance. It seems as though everyone wants your body or your money but nobody wants you. As some singles shared with me, "You feel that, except for sex and a good time, you are a disposable person to be used, then dumped."

*Even our strugglers are way ahead of the average person "out there."* In the Christian community we understand that people are not to be used. The book of James tells us that every person is created in the image of God (see 3:9). We know that the best way to treat another human being is to respect God's revealed absolutes. Lying, stealing, getting high, having sex outside of marriage are not okay. They are destructive to people and their relationships. Most of the post-Christian culture in America no longer believes in scriptural absolutes and, as a result, people and relationships are being destroyed on a wholesale basis.

The earlier generation of secular humanists often were products of an evangelical heritage. They themselves no longer believed in the inspiration or authority of Scripture but they accepted many scriptural absolutes of their fathers as good standards by which to live. But their children asked, "Why bother? Why not just do our thing if no binding truth exists?" And suddenly the gates opened wide to a universal demolition of personhood.

This means that we in the evangelical church have a commodity necessary to an unstable society. We have people who understand absolutes and live by unchanging values. Even our strugglers are miles ahead of the average unchurched person. That makes the fortress mentality of keeping to ourselves all the more disastrous and all the more sinful. Our culture needs us. They need groups like our singles to provide an alternative to other movements which are floundering in a values vacuum.

*It's true; they really do need us.* Foreign student advisors also need our people. When our International Student leadership first spoke to some of them about our work, the advisors were understandably wary. If our people just wanted to dump Christianity on these students we could forget it. We assured them that such was not the case. Our goal was to build positive relationships with foreign students and share who we are as Americans, but also as Christians.

They assigned a few students to our host families and waited to get the students' reactions. Some of these were Iranian students coming in the wake of Khomeni's capture of American hostages. When they discovered that we didn't hate them, that we would in fact go the extra mile to help them, they went back to their advisors with glowing reports. So the advisors sent more students. Soon they were asking us to find more families. Their message changed from being afraid of us to being eager for more of us to become involved.

We have gotten the same word from state and county agencies concerning our girls' home. They have seen that a degree in social work doesn't necessarily prepare its recipient to be a good model for delinquent kids. When counselors who are graduates of the situational ethics school come to work and talk about smoking pot or sleeping around or getting drunk, they present the same destructive images the girls had in their troubled homes or out on the streets. The kids whom the state has taken into their custody need different models than the secular humanists are providing. In contrast, it's amazing how well a healthy, consistent, but non-oppressive Christian environment works in our girls' home. We in no way force Christianity on the girls in the home we operate. But daily our staff models what it means to be Christ-ones. Runaways decrease, the hostility level drops, and the girls function better. As a result we have received several letters from the state and surrounding counties asking us to consider opening more homes.

Our street house, too, is almost always at capacity. We have turned away hundreds of people. True, many are just looking for a handout but others really want an alternative to the street scene.

We have found we are needed out there beyond the fortress. We have something to offer. We have people who have God's love in their hearts for everyone and who also have an unchanging system of values. This is a rare commodity in post-Christian America. Singles, street people, foreign student advisors and local government officials know it is difficult to find.

### The Average Church Has All It Needs for a Major Ministry

The real tragedy is that while the demand is high for our people outside the fortress, we have them boxed in. We have developed an inferiority complex, believing no one would respond to us if we tried to minister outside our fortress. We have our lay people tied up and constricted by church busywork, or we have persuaded them that they are primarily spectators. Only those people who have degrees from Christian schools actually do the ministry; for everyone else it's, "Be sure to be in your place when the meeting starts." Ugh!

We don't have to have big facilities or be on television to have an impact on our cities. We have all we need if we have Christ-ones who are committed to reaching others. These people have values; they understand absolutes and the love of Christ flows through them. They just need to be unleashed,

When they are, people on the outside will say, "We need more like you." The unleashed Christians will return to the church meetings from their ministries alive with a New Testament dynamic. They will lead people to Christ and attract other believers to this unusual ministering church and soon there will be more "just like us" to send into the community to minister.

For the church to be unleashed, we need to understand that "it's true—they really do need us." But we also need to look within the church body and see the tensions that exist between spirit and structure. We may have people with the love of Christ in their hearts and an absolute values system to live by, but if we structure them out of the community they will never make contact with the throngs of people who need them.

### Notes

1. Dr. Vernon Grounds, *HIS*, August 1980, p. 40.
2. "Where Is Jerry Falwell Going?" *Eternity*, July-August 1980, p. 20.
3. See Philippians 1:17, King James Version.

## Chapter 5

# Spirit Versus Structure

The man on the other end of the telephone was making a difficult request. He wanted to know whether Bear Valley would sponsor five Hmong refugee families out of Laos. The situation was urgent. The families were in an apartment complex, but for some reason had neither sponsors nor immediate access to government money. When the apartment owner became aware of their predicament he wanted them out immediately.

I told my caller that I didn't know if we could help or not but I would find out and let him know that evening. I then called the leaders of several Sunday School classes and some "Caring Units." They, in turn, checked with their people and by evening we had five sponsoring groups. Later the caller told me he knew of only two churches in the city which were structured to be able to respond quickly to this kind of request. Of course he didn't know every church in the city, but the Christian community has come to expect most churches to take a month or more to respond to needs outside the church. As the refrain goes, "Like a mighty glacier moves the church of God."

### Ministry Opportunities Can't Always Wait

As a result of our ability to respond quickly we were able to move the families out of the complex within a few days. Our people invested a lot of time in helping them get relocated. We soon discovered that a couple of the families were Christians. Then God led us to a young Christian Hmong who had been trained by missionaries in Laos. He spoke excellent English and agreed to become our translator. We gave him some financial help so he could spend several hours a week ministering to his own people. Soon fifty to sixty Hmong were attending one of our services. They shared in the opening with us; then during the sermon they went into a separate room and one of our pastors taught them through the interpreter.

Within a year the Hmong moved to a facility provided by the Southern Baptists. Some later left to form a church with the denomination that had worked with them in Laos, the Christian Missionary Alliance. Two strong churches have resulted from those first five families, and we have continued to work with the churches in their new locations.

The ability of our church to respond quickly to such opportunities, as well as our involvement with numerous other target groups, springs from the convictions that are discussed in this chapter.

### The Gospel Is the Essence of the Church

We have an understanding in our ministry: if we become aware of a gospel need and have the resources to meet that need, the answer is yes. In the refugee case, the question of whether or not we should help did not need to be referred to a committee or a church business meeting. Of course we should help if we can. What determines whether or not we can help? In this, and in most cases, the biggest need is people's time. Some ministries require large amounts of money but most do not. When the need is primarily people, then it is simple. If we have the people we will undertake the ministry—if not, we won't.

Several months ago one of our pastors received a call from Italy asking us to sponsor two Russian refugees. The people in Italy had expected another church to be their sponsors. But at the last moment, before they were scheduled to leave for the United States, the other church declined to accept the sponsorship. In this case there was potentially a few thousand dollars involved in the commitment. Pastor Thompson knew he had to ask a larger group than a Sunday School class so he went directly to one of the congregations he pastors and they committed themselves to provide whatever was needed. Within a week we were able to have the couple on their way. The two refugees have been in the United States several months now. They have become a part of the congregation that sponsored them.

These types of ministries are the natural result of understanding the essence of the church to be gospel. If there is a particular gospel need presented to us and we have the gospel resources to meet that need, then we will do so. This has delivered our ministry from the "committee-grind."

*A different perspective on committees.* In our approach to ministry we have moved away from the traditional use of committees. What purpose do most committees serve? First, they decide whether someone in the church ought to do something or not. We have already decided that question. If there is a gospel need and we have gospel resources to meet that need, the answer is yes. After the decision has been made to become involved, the committee must then move on to their second function, which is answering the question, "Who can we get to do it?" This method has the built-in dilemma of someone deciding something should be done, then trying to find someone else to do it. Of course, finding someone to do it is often difficult because many of the best people are serving on other committees and are too busy looking for people to do things for them. As a result, potentially productive people are tied up in a bureaucratic machine.

When I first came to Bear Valley there were over twenty committees on the books. Fortunately, there weren't enough people to fill them so they were all nonfunctional. The only functioning group was the board of deacons. When the deacons interviewed me I assured them that I didn't intend to make quick changes or demands. But I would have to insist on one thing before I accepted the position of pastor: we had to commit ourselves to becoming a ministering church. We wouldn't have time to maintain a bureaucracy; that meant no standing committees. All budget and housekeeping matters were to be managed by the deacons. Of course we would have open financial records and regular reports to the church and since we were a church under congregational rule we would have to have large, non-budgeted expenditures approved by the church. The deacons would meet for business matters once a month. This has meant that our people don't get bogged down in the machinery of organization.

When we get together it is for fellowship, prayer or ministry.

That doesn't mean we are committed to a no-structure approach. In fact we're very concerned about the balance between spirit and structure in the church. We are aware of how structure emerged in the New Testament. In Acts 6, structure was needed, so they developed it. Our commitment isn't to nonstructure, but rather to structure that is the result of ministry. Each Sunday School class that accepted the responsibility of sponsoring a refugee family had to decide on a structure that would get the job done. They were free to work in whatever manner they chose. Some decided to get the entire class involved. Others asked for two or three families to volunteer to do the whole job. In each case the classes were prepared to respond because the class leadership had checked with several key people who said, "Yes, let's do it." In doing this they carried out both necessary functions of a committee. First, they decided the question of whether we should do it or not; second, they committed *themselves* to actually carrying it out.

If we have people to do the ministry, the structure of that ministry will take care of itself. If we don't have the people there is no sense in frustrating a committee with the task of finding people who aren't there.

While Bear Valley is not committee-oriented, we really have many kinds of committees functioning. They are not, however, standing, elected committees. They have "emerged" out of a call to minister. In effect they are ministry teams, groups of people who have said, "Yes, we should do it" and "Yes, we will do it." This gives our committees the tremendous advantage of internal motivation so often lacking in the traditional approach. That is to say, our committees, or ministry teams, have a high degree of want-to.

We have seen several ministries conceived, born, established and maintained for years strictly by lay people. There is no annual beating the drums to fill the slots that for some reason we imagine must be filled. Rather, highly motivated people plan a structure and work within that structure because they want to.

*The Holy Spirit can and will shape the church as He pleases.* Once we do away with the structure-first approach we are free to allow the Holy Spirit to shape us. The structure-first approach is one in which the structure is set and whatever ministry it spits out, the church does. That's much different from a ministry-first approach. This approach says that if we have the people who want to perform a certain ministry, we will build a structure around them.

One of the saddest commentaries on the evangelical church is its deadening sameness. One can look in the yellow pages and find Sunday School, worship, Sunday evening and midweek services listed with numbing regularity. If the church is one of the 37,000 Southern Baptist churches you can also expect to find Women's Missionary Union, Brotherhood, Girls' Auxiliary, Royal Ambassadors and Training Union. If it is not Southern Baptist, look for basically the same groups with different names. When Detroit mass-produces, all the models come off the assembly line looking the same. When the Holy Spirit creates, each one is unique. Everything God creates is one of a kind. Yes, there are similarities between snowflakes and fingerprints. Yes, we should expect similarities among evangelical churches, but not the sameness which suffocates.

Recently, I was visiting the town in which I grew up. I was saddened by the news that two churches which had always been faithful to preach the gospel were closing down. As I was out jogging I ran by both of their buildings. The signs in front advertised 9:45 Sunday School, 11:00 Worship, 7:00 P.M. Evening Service and 7:30 P.M. Wednesday Evening Prayer Service. These churches chose to die, rather than change. I am grateful that they did not change their message to stay alive, but they could have changed their methods.

How does the Holy Spirit shape a living church? There is undoubtedly a many-faceted answer to that question. But I'm convinced He shapes primarily through people. The Antioch church became the greatest missionary church in the New Testament because God gave them the greatest missionaries. As a church we too are convinced that we should be doing whatever it is the Holy Spirit has laid on the hearts of the people whom He has sent to us.

When I visit someone who is interested in our church, I never look at that person as a candidate to plug a hole in a program. These people are often surprised when I tell them that we are as open to structuring around them in a new venture as we are to having them get involved in an already established work. They are always encouraged to share their dreams for ministry with one of the pastors. And we rarely discourage them from going ahead with that ministry.

One of the newest ministries in our church is a health-care ministry. The woman who heads it recently graduated with a degree in Health-Care Management. Because of her husband's income she can invest her time in volunteer work. And she felt she should use her time to explore a health-care ministry. One has only to look at the Seventh-Day Adventists to see some of the possibilities in this field. So she advertised such a ministry in the church bulletin and held an open meeting for anyone interested. Several people showed up. Some were health-care professionals; others were interested in holistic health and nutrition. (Such initial brainstorming sessions are usually attended and conducted by lay people only. The pastors do not necessarily feel a need to be there unless they are going to be directly involved in the ministry.)

A second health-care meeting held shortly afterward produced a smaller group. These became the core people and they began to map out the structure of the ministry. The first visible evidence of their work in the church was a class on "Nutritional Cooking for One or Two." Where this health-care ministry will go in the future remains to be seen. It will depend on the people God sends into the ministry, what He puts on their hearts, and the needs they see. The shape of this ministry, as well as the whole church, is simple: the Holy Spirit leads people and people shape the Body.

A ministry that recently surfaced, but which has been put on the shelf for now, is a roller-skating ministry. A young couple felt led to investigate the possibility of renting a roller rink twice a month for a ministry to unchurched junior highers. The idea has a lot of possibilities, but at this moment the Lord has not supplied either a rink or the necessary workers. In such cases we simply relax until the Holy Spirit fits the necessary pieces together.

When I first came to Bear Valley, for example, I had a special burden for singles. My wife, Mary, and I had worked with singles at another church. We longed to see a singles ministry at Bear Valley. For six years we prayed and waited. Then a couple who had felt the agony of divorce were led to begin a singles class. Within a few months another member of the church became available to join our staff. We hired him, moved the singles class into a restaurant and in a short time this ministry became one of the most significant in the church. Once again God's timing was evident. We are not primarily concerned about starting new ministries or programs. Our concern is to discern God's moving in our church and to get in step with Him. If we have to wait six or ten years for a ministry to begin, that's okay. But when God moves people, our structure must not be in the way.

### Lay People Can Be Trusted with Ministry

A basic assumption in this approach to ministry is that lay people are capable of planning and carrying on a ministry. The church unleashed will look to the laity for ministry in a primary way. Ephesians 4:11,12 talks about God giving pastor-teachers to the church to equip the laity to do the work of the ministry. That must be taken seriously, since there are so many more lay people and they can do so much more ministry. The pattern of Scripture is clear: pastor-teachers are to train lay men and women to minister to the world. They in turn are to train others and the work continues.

Our churches are full of highly trained, mature believers. Many have been trained in parachurch organizations, Bible colleges or seminaries. Others have been students of the Word for years. Yet we are so often structured to major on giving them more information about the Bible and the Christian life. They are taught in Sunday School, in the morning and evening worship services, and often again in midweek. They need ministry opportunities where they can put to work the content they are absorbing. Believers are to be vitally involved in presenting the message of freedom in Christ to a world imprisoned (see Isa. 40).

Many of our lay people are much more capable of putting together and maintaining ministries than we pastors think they are. As I have already mentioned, many of our ministries are conceived, born and nurtured by lay people. These are not only target-group ministries, they include many traditional ministries which the staff does not feel it can or should do.

For several years we did not have a Vacation Bible School. When people asked why, we replied that the Body had not produced anyone to organize and direct a VBS. Three years ago one of our members said she wanted to conduct a Bible school. She met a few times with our pastor of Christian education but she took full responsibility for the ministry and did a tremendous job. I am convinced that many more lay people will accomplish great tasks when they become convinced that we pastors are serious about allowing them to do the ministry.

*The greater the relationship, the fewer the rules.* What I have been describing will be difficult for many vocational and lay leaders in the church to accept. This style of ministry lessens their control. Unfortunately church leaders, vocational and lay, are often not accustomed to trusting people with ministry. I will return to the matter of trust again in the chapter on pastoral leadership. At this point I want to make it clear that the church unleashed is built on trust and trust is built on relationships.

Howard Hendricks, the popular conference speaker, speaking about his relationship with his wife, says that he and his wife have no rules in their marriage. They have no rules because they have such a great relationship. They're convinced that "the greater the relationship, the fewer the rules." The church unleashed also needs to be built on great relationships, both the vertical relationship of believers to their Lord, and their horizontal relationships with one another. When lay people confide in us pastors that they believe God is calling them into a certain ministry, we trust them. We feel responsible to encourage and help them if we can, but they must take the responsibility of doing the ministry. The key factors are always trust and responsibility.

If you were to visit one of our weekly staff meetings you would discover an informal time devoted to the vertical and horizontal relationships of our people. At present we have four congregations, four Sunday School sessions and a variety of ministries. Yet we spend very little time in programs. Our main concern is, "How is so-and-so doing? How is he progressing in his spiritual life? Is he getting along with other people?" We major on relationships because we know that the greater the relationships, the fewer the rules. If people have right relationships they can be trusted with ministry.

*The Body can be trusted to produce what it needs.* The passages of Scripture in which Paul describes the Body give us an amazing picture of the delicate, interdependent working of all the parts. The Head of the Body, according to Ephesians 1:22,23, is the Lord Jesus Christ. He can be trusted to work through His Body in such a supernatural way that the Body will produce what it needs. Just as the physical body may produce more than its usual strength or speed in certain crisis situations, the spiritual Body of the church can be trusted to produce what it needs, when it needs it.

This can be seen in many ways at Bear Valley. Perhaps one of the best illustrations is the development of the many types of small groups. When we began the alternate congregations we decided to have ninety-minute worship services without adult Sunday Schools. Instead, adults who were interested would meet in homes during the week in Caring Units. People in the traditional congregations heard about the caring units and decided that they too wanted to be in a small home group. But they knew that the caring-unit structure wasn't right for them. So after reading a book by Louis Evans entitled *Creative Love*,[1] the first of several covenant groups was formed. We now have caring units, covenant groups, Bible studies, prayer groups, Navigator 2:7 Discipleship Groups, and who knows what else. Small groups are allowed to form and die as the needs of the Body dictate. We have never had any of the feared heresy, rebellion or immorality usually predicted for such loosely controlled groups. We realized from the beginning that we would be taking risks if we didn't keep a tight rein on our people. But we chose to trust the Body to produce what it needed. As it turned out, the risk was small, the dividends huge.

## Spirit and Structure in Balance—The Creative Tension

The issue of spirit and structure is a crucial one. It's not a question of either/or; rather, it is a question of priority. Most churches have given the priority to structure. That makes sense when we recall our heritage. This defensive mind-set is a result of the modernist-fundamentalist controversy. Because of this controversy most evangelical churches have majored on being sure their people think correctly. To be sure they did think in the right way, a trusted leader had to be in all the church meetings. As a result, lay people have become conditioned to think that they had better not, or that they are unable to start a ministry or lead a study. After all, they might not do it right.

What then is such a church to do with its lay people? It must build elaborate housekeeping committees to get them involved. But it dare not let them become involved in or lead the ministries; they might sell out to the liberals or the cults. Hence, fearful pastors direct their vitality and strength into a strictly controlled and "safe" series of programs.

Structure has become the enemy of the church unleashed. I agree with Howard Snyder when he says: "Protestantism is caught in a stifling web of institutionalism. The wineskins have grown rigid. It is not enough, therefore, merely to call for change or to proclaim the need. The whole problem of wineskins—the *structure* of the church—must be dealt with."[2]

I have already mentioned the need for spirit to precede structure. But once this priority is established we must then pursue structure diligently. The Holy Spirit does not call the church to sloppiness or anarchy. When He leads into a ministry, we must build an appropriate structure around it. We need to know, for example, who is responsible, what the objectives are, what physical resources are needed, who is going to supply them, etc. There must be a creative tension between the working of the Holy Spirit and the structure of our ministries. If an atmosphere of chaos prevails and things are not being done "decently and in order," it is likely that spirit has eaten up structure. But if the problem is a listless committee on which people serve because no one else will do it, it is likely that structure has devoured spirit. Our aim is a creative tension between the two with spirit leading the way and structure enabling the effectiveness of our ministries.

Sometimes the interplay between spirit and structure can be nerve-racking or faith-stretching. A few years ago four couples in one of our caring units read Ron Sider's *Rich Christians in an Age of Hunger*.[3] They then decided they wanted to give a total of $600 per month over their present commitments to the church to be used for a street ministry. That same week my nephew from Memphis, Tennessee called me. He had been working with street people there for several years. On one occasion, some time before, I had mentioned to him that we would like to see the Lord lead us into a similar ministry. And now, suddenly, here he was on the telephone confiding that he felt, for some reason, that God wanted him to move to Denver and begin a street work. I shared with him what our couples had just committed themselves to do and, of course, we both became more and more excited as we saw how the pieces of this particular puzzle were falling together.

After he visited us in Denver and met the supporting couples we made a mutual agreement that he would come. It was a difficult decision. A street ministry requires considerably more money than $600 per month. But God had clearly put everything together to that point and the four couples and I were confident He wanted us to keep moving.

So my nephew and his wife made plans to come, and we prayed for more provision to begin the street work. We already knew that this particular ministry could almost pay its own way once it was firmly established, since a work program was planned as an integral part of the ministry. That planned structure for the street ministry has since proven to be effective and practical. The work program supplies money for the street house so that it has not become just another welfare program. It also provides an opportunity to teach discipline, work skills, team work and responsibility—all of which are in short supply for most street people. But in those earliest stages of the ministry money was needed to rent and equip a house, perhaps lease a gas station or buy janitorial equipment. We didn't feel we could ask the church to help in such a large venture since several other ministries had recently been funded over and above the budget.

With what we thought to be certain evidence, however, that this ministry was of the Lord and was within His timing, the church hired our street pastor. Shortly after he arrived, the church received a special gift from two Christian businessmen whom I had never met. One of our members, an investor, was raising money to purchase a building from these two men. He told them about how God had begun to bring this ministry together. And they, seeing the enormous possibilities of such a work, responded with a gift of $50,000. The building they sold was called the Genesis Building; hence, we named our street house the Genesis Center.

God honored our trust. It wasn't blind trust because He had already clearly begun to work. But He waited for us to take a major step of faith before He put the final pieces together.

Too often a ministry that puts structure before spirit cannot take that step. Bureaucrats are not in the habit of moving ahead on faith. They usually want to secure every possible need before ever committing themselves to any project.

The tension between spirit and structure in the church is crucial. If spirit eats up structure, the resulting chaos will be neither productive for nor honoring to God. If structure eats up spirit, the resulting orderly deadness will make a mockery of what is supposed to be the dynamic Body of Christ. While it's not a matter of either/or, it is important that the spirit have priority. Structure should stay flexible; the skin must shape itself to the new wine.

### The Value of Maintaining a Traditional Base

Elton Trueblood's book, *The Company of the Committed*, published in 1961 signaled the beginning of a wave of books on church renewal. Many of these books have had a far-reaching and positive impact on churches in the United States and around the world. But on the other hand, many conveyed ideas that are not workable in a traditional church structure. And as a result their renewal principles are not being used by many churches.

At Bear Valley we feel strongly that the church unleashed is best built on a traditional structural base. I believe that most candidates for full-time vocational ministry are still becoming Christians in Sunday School, Vacation Bible School or at youth camps, etc. Furthermore, there is something very special for many people in a worship service that has well-prepared special music and quality accompanists. To have that dimension in a worship service you must have a serious music program. To have a quality Sunday School you must have serious teachers and a high level commitment from both the church staff and the church budget.

At Bear Valley we have, at present, two traditional worship services and two alternate worship services. We never think of them in terms of better or worse, just different. But it has been interesting to see the traditional congregations grow the faster. The church unleashed is not intended to be a radical attack on the traditional church structure. Apart from the normal use of committees the church unleashed does not need to do away with the traditional dimensions of the ministry; instead it builds upon them. A church with a small facility and a traditional structure has a great foundation upon which to build.

So far we've been talking about the mind-sets and attitudes of the church unleashed. But what about the physical plant? What role do church buildings play? The question is of much debate and great importance.

**Notes**
1. Louis H. Evans, *Creative Love* (Old Tappan, NJ: Fleming H. Revell, Co., 1978).
2. Howard A. Snyder, *The Problem of Wineskins* (Downers Grove, IL: Inter-Varsity Press, 1975), pp. 50,51.
3. Ronald J. Sider, *Rich Christians in an Age of Hunger* (Downers Grove, IL: Inter-Varsity Press, 1977).

## Chapter 6

# A Major Ministry with Modest Facilities

As we looked at the plot of land it wasn't difficult to see the possibilities. There were several acres for building and parking. It was located on one major street and very near another. The area around it was booming with new apartment complexes and housing developments. Our church was growing; we were holding double services. A move to a choice spot like this seemed the natural thing to do.

Most growing churches we knew of had filled their buildings to "capacity," then moved to more land at the edge of the city. Or some had acquired enough land in the beginning to build additional facilities where they were. But we didn't have that extra space. In fact we had just a little over one acre and there were churches on either side of us, which meant our street parking was limited.

Many felt we needed more room, much more room; but some of us were uneasy about responding to growth in this typical way. We were reluctant to move deeper into suburbia and assume a large mortgage. Yet we knew we had to do something. The church had been growing steadily but in the past year we had gone into decline. The parking lot was jammed, nurseries overcrowded and people sensed the leadership was undecided about what to do.

Most of us were convinced that our growth would explode if we moved and built a much bigger facility. At the same time we were thinking that there must be a wiser choice. Somehow we should be able to stay in our small building and still continue to grow. We spent hours in staff meetings, deacons' meetings and church meetings pondering the question.

We decided to stay and eventually remodel our present facility. It is important to note that once we decided to stay, we began to discover several creative alternatives to help us continue to grow in a small, poor facility.

People who study church growth say a five-percent increase per year over a decade is good growth. The percentage at Bear Valley had been twenty percent per year over a nine-year period. During that time we had to work with our less-than-adequate facility. The building originally had been built on a shoestring. Walls curved where they weren't supposed to; restrooms were tiny; the nursery was hopelessly overcrowded. The sanctuary couldn't be enlarged much; our staying would commit us to a maximum congregation of approximately 300.

Looking back now, that decision to stay was one of the best we ever made. True, we might be a larger church today if we had moved, but we also would have been plagued with all the liabilities of a large facility.

As it turned out, our inadequate conditions did not keep us from growing. And any church in the city with modest facilities can also grow to many times the number of people they presently serve.

There are thousands of evangelical churches in America's cities with facilities about the size of ours. At one time they were in a new suburban development, but growth has long since passed them by. We look at the churches which have continued to grow over the years and see basically the same pattern; grow until you have your present facility nearly full or for double services; then rally the people around a big building program. Either you buy land toward an expanding edge of town or (if money is no object) near a freeway intersection. In either case you then build a much larger, more elaborate plant. Of course if you have sufficient land or can buy more land around the original church, your facility can always expand at its present site.

But if a church is unable to implement one of the foregoing options, it seems it must resign itself to a constricting facility, admit defeat and settle for never expanding beyond the present capacity of its building.

There is, however, another option. We need not choose between more land and bigger buildings or a small, limited ministry. We can build a major ministry in a modest facility. In fact, this option may be the best choice for most churches. This is not to say that it is the only choice. Every city needs evangelical churches with big facilities. These churches are equipped for ministries the rest of us cannot handle. But it's wrong when these super plants become the primary model for all growing, struggling churches. It's wrong for two major reasons. First, most city churches with small facilities will never be able to buy prime land and build large facilities. Second, the big-facility ministry engenders certain subtle liabilities which would be best avoided, even if we could afford land and buildings. Let's talk about how the assets of a small facility can offset these potential dangers.

## Modest Facilities Force Us to Creative Decentralization

The fortress church thinks it important to keep its ministry located in "God's house." The church unleashed is eager to move its bases of ministry out of the church building to become "God's host" in an inhospitable, hostile world. With our small facility we simply cannot base all of our ministries in the building, and that's fine. After all, the church got along without church buildings until the third century. If someone had asked a believer in Philippi, "Where is the church?" he certainly never would have answered 2600 South Sheridan Boulevard! The church was everywhere the believers were, and it still is.

If the parachurch ministries have taught us anything, it is that we don't necessarily have to have a church building to have an effective ministry.

Decentralizing the ministry can force us to be creative. As I mentioned earlier, we wanted to have a singles ministry for a number of years. We only had a small Sunday School classroom and somehow the atmosphere in the church building just didn't seem conducive to reaching singles. The atmosphere was right for middle-class family units but singles didn't seem to fit very well. Even if the atmosphere had been right, there was just too little space.

About that time I heard Ray Stedman of the

Peninsula Bible Church of Palo Alto, California,
speak. He mentioned that he had recently wit-
nessed the baptism of a large number of singles.
He went on to explain that they had over 1,000
singles meeting in four restaurants in the San
Francisco Bay area. I felt as though I had been
slapped on the side of the head and told to wake
up! We moved our singles class to a nearby restaurant. And as soon as we did, we began to grow
both spiritually and numerically. We now have
ministries targeted not only toward singles, but
also toward street people, delinquent girls, international students and senior citizens—all based
outside the fortress.

In addition many of our homes have become
bases for ministry. Not only do groups meet in
homes but several individuals who, for some reason have no home of their own, live with our
church families. We anticipate that this decentralizing process has just begun. The freedom to
think decentralization continually releases unlimited creative possibilities.

### Modest Facilities Help People Stay Visible
People often ask, "Is Bear Valley four different
churches or one church in four congregations?"
The answer is the latter. (Some day we may be one
church in eight congregations.) The next question
is usually, "How in the world do people know each
other if these congregations attend worship services at four different times?" That's a good question. The answer is two-fold. First, our people do a
number of things together apart from the worship
services. A lot of overlapping occurs in the ministries and other activities of the church. Second,
and more important, the question of missed relationships presupposes that if a large number of

people attend a worship service together they will somehow get to know one another. I am not aware of any studies which can provide data on this question, but I suspect that once the size of any group exceeds 250 to 300 it becomes increasingly difficult to know all within that group. After that it doesn't matter if more people attend at the same time or not; the majority simply do not have the capacity to even casually know more than 300 people at one time.

We had to educate our people concerning the illusion that they might get acquainted with more people if they all worshiped at the same time. Once they realized that there were enough people in their particular congregation to keep them at "knowing capacity," the "fractured church" they had feared was no longer an issue.

Rather than losing opportunities for knowing people by limiting each service to 300, we actually gain the ability to know better the people in our particular congregation. Individuals are more visible in a group of 300 than they are in a group of 1,000. This is tremendously important. For in the city we are swallowed up in crowds wherever we go. We are anonymous in shopping centers, at ball games, driving through congested streets; but in our congregations, people know us. We find identity there within the intimacy of the Body.

You might ask the question, "If people are usually anonymous in the city, won't they feel more comfortable remaining anonymous in the church? Are we working against the 'urban psyche' here?" The answer to both questions in this case is yes. Many in the city go to churches with big auditoriums filled with people, in order to remain unnoticed and uninvolved. But when the "urban psyche" directly conflicts with our ability to help people to realize their full stature in Christ, we must work against it.

The objective of small congregational units, however, is not to make the Sunday gathering a time when only a few are present. City people don't usually feel comfortable in a small public gathering. Our family recently went to dinner at a popular restaurant. We had to wait half an hour to be seated. We were much more comfortable in that setting than if we had entered a restaurant at mealtime and only a few other people were there. The city person feels comfortable with large numbers of people. Some of our congregations overlap; others are coming in as another group is leaving. We think it is an advantage to have our congregations meet as they come and go, but then when their worship service begins, the group is small enough so that everyone is visible.

### Modest Facilities Deliver Us from the Spectator-Performer Syndrome

As Richard Halverson discovered, in a congregation of over 7,000 only 365 had jobs to do. This seems to say that the majority of the membership of large churches feel responsible merely to show up when the professionals are doing their thing. Lay people have been programmed to watch what is going on up front. The bigger the facility, the bigger the performance. The bigger the facility, the greater the distance between the person in the pulpit and the people in the congregation. Most of us have yet to grasp the consequences of the churches' gravitation toward the superstar mentality. The evangelical performance has become the norm. We have conditioned people to think that the successful Christian worker performs his or her ministry in front of great numbers of people. The vast majority of people in our churches don't have that opportunity, so they think, "It's best to leave the ministry to the professionals."

What a shame that in a day when our cities cry out for the touch of Christ, when they so need our evangelical people "out there," that Christians sit week after week in their pews, mesmerized by one big performance after another.

A small facility cannot cure this spectator-performer syndrome by itself, but it can suggest the healthy message: "Anybody can minister here." Such a small facility must be coupled with a large ministry; otherwise, we merely have the big-fish-in-a-little-pond problem. As long as one or two leaders can do most of the speaking and most of the counseling, and oversee most of the ministries, the vision of the church is too limited. And this is exactly what is happening in many of our smaller churches. On the other hand, if the facility is small but the ministry is large, the church will be forced to develop more vocational and lay leadership.

### Modest Facilities Allow Us to Spend More Money on People

It's an often quoted fact that the United States has six percent of the world's population but consumes forty percent of its natural resources. Nobody needs to be told that those resources are becoming scarce and that the price tag is going up astronomically. These scarcities are daily producing changes in our society. American automobile makers are in a terrible quandary because they failed to see in time the demand for small economical cars. American churches will soon be in a similar predicament if we insist on constructing buildings large enough to contain everyone at the same time. Expenses are rapidly becoming prohibitive. Land, building materials, interest rates, inflation and energy costs are strangling already overextended budgets. Many financial experts are predicting the day when the utility bill will equal the mortgage payment. Furthermore, once a building has been constructed it must be maintained. In today's economy a crew of janitors requires a small fortune. Such financial burdens will certainly force churches to look at the small facility with a new appreciation.

Ralph Neighbour, in *The Seven Last Words of the Church*, makes some important observations about the churches' dependence on buildings: "Churches in the United States now own in excess of $102 billion in land and buildings. I am not picking on my denomination, but simply using it as an example: We will spend far more than $50 million this year *simply to pay the interest on church mortgages*. This profit by bankers from churches represents an investment which is several million dollars more than the amount to be invested by those churches for all home and foreign mission causes."[1]

No wonder Stephen Board says, "In influence and money—that is, in *power*—the parachurch agencies are running away with the ball game."[2] The parachurch doesn't have its money tied up in nonproductive church buildings. Their dollars are channeled toward people ministries and their contributors appreciate that. They want their contributions to be productive and so invest them in productive ministries out in the community.

There is something exciting about ministering to a thousand people while having building maintenance costs for only 300. Especially when we know that we can at least double our number in the same facility. And then when we reach that goal we can begin planting churches elsewhere. With this vision in mind we are confident that our small facility will never prevent us from growing.

We are often asked how a church like ours can run so many ministries and hire so many staff members. We are certainly not a wealthy church. But since our money is not locked into maintaining a large facility, we can channel it into missions, local ministry and additional staff.

We have a long way to go in the evangelical community to restore credibility in our local churches in the areas of building and finance. True, some churches with large facilities are using them to the maximum throughout the week; however, the vast majority of church buildings, large or small, most of the time sit useless and empty.

In light of the tremendous expense of building and maintaining facilities, Neighbour has an important insight: "The population of the United States will probably double in the next 30 years, requiring my denomination alone to double the number of local churches—*just to stay equal in witness to what we are doing today.* My denomination began church building programs in 1845. In 125 years it has amassed 35,000 units; now, it must erect 35,000 more in only 30 years to stay even."[3] Neighbour highlights the church's impossible task. It must either change its financial practices or spend a larger percentage of its budget for buildings.

### Small Facilities Allow Us to Have an Occasional Big Event as a Change of Pace

The small facility, as has been noted, helps to deliver us from a spectator-performer mentality. That is especially true when a small facility is coupled with a large ministry. Yet it does not prevent us from occasionally bringing everyone together for a big united event. For this purpose we have, at separate times, utilized a large Seventh-Day Adventist church and a high school auditorium to bring all the congregations together, combine the choirs, show slides of the various ministries and serve a large potluck dinner. This provides all congregations opportunity for encouraging one another, sharing their vision, and renewing their enthusiasm for ministry. This also furnishes an occasion for members to bring visitors who want to get a complete picture of the church's ministries.

We have seen that when a church has a large facility its people are usually programmed to expect great performances each week. But in a church that is ministry—not meeting—oriented, they come to appreciate the big event as an exception, rather than the rule.

### Modest Facilities with Major Ministries Demand More Leadership

The only way a church can grow in small facilities is to multiply its groups. As the groups multiply, their leadership must also multiply, including even the pastor-teacher. Here again our churches have wandered away from the biblical pattern of multiple elders or pastors. The "one-man show" is not found in the New Testament; the church is a participatory body. The pastor-teacher is to set the example of "teaching others who will be able to teach others also." For if everyone sits under the teaching of only one pastor, there will never be opportunity to develop the co-pastors which a larger ministry requires. There will be plenty of room for assistants, but not for true co-pastors. A growing ministry in a small facility will soon demand more than double services. The senior pastor will then face a marathon of meetings each Sunday or he will have to allow someone else to become the main pastor-teacher of a separate congregation.

Will people go to a service when someone other than the senior pastor is the pastor-teacher? We will discuss the role of senior pastor and questions such as this in more detail in the next chapter. For the purpose of our discussion at this point we need to point out that people will sit under the preaching of another pastor if two things happen.

The first is that the senior pastor must encourage people to go to that other congregation. He must assure them that he won't take their leaving personally. He must take the responsibility of educating the people to the projected change long before it ever happens and show them from the Scripture the basis for a multiple-pastor ministry. The second thing is more difficult to put into words. The church unleashed will have an easier time developing true co-pastors than the fortress church because it is not big-meeting oriented. Rather, the primary orientation will be toward the various ministries of the Body. Therefore, in the church unleashed, people will come to the services eager to be fed from the Word and to worship with other believers. Sunday worship will provide a time of refreshment and renewal for Christians who have been giving of themselves to others during the week. If the emphasis is on corporate worship rather than on the performance of a superstar with oral accompaniment, the congregation will find it easier to accept another pastor-teacher.

Developing more leadership may begin with the position of pastor-teacher, but it goes far beyond that. It extends to Sunday School teachers, music ministry leaders, plus the many types of leadership positions not normally found in the fortress church. The people must understand that this is not pragmatic only; it is a biblical pattern which God will bless if we follow His direction.

Because our facility is small, we do not have room for large Sunday School classes. In fact, the way we use our facility for the two alternate congregations eliminates the possibility of having adult Sunday School classes at all. In the case of the two traditional congregations, we are forced to create more classes which means we must have more leadership. In the alternate congregations we are forced to go outside the main facility and minister to adults in homes during the week. Instead of Sunday School classes, the alternate congregations have developed Caring Units. Caring Units are close-knit small groups; the average number in a unit is ten. That means the same number of people who would normally be under the leadership of a single teacher in a Sunday School class of fifty needs five leaders when divided into Caring Units.

The Caring Unit has also allowed us to develop a different type of leader from the Sunday School teacher. Caring Units are led by lay pastors. We train a lay pastor to be the main pastor of his unit. On alternate Saturday mornings, lay pastors gather for two hours of instruction in theology, counseling and effective communication. They are expected to provide or to train others to provide most of the pastoral ministries for their units.

We can develop a different type of leader in a Caring Unit than we can in a Sunday School class because Caring Units are closed. People must have permission to visit a Caring Unit and they must have a high level of commitment to join one. We are not trying to develop that same context in Sunday School classes. Sunday School is a part of the public gathering on Sunday; therefore, the classes need to be open for visitors or those with a low-level commitment. That doesn't mean Sunday School is a second-class ministry, but it does mean the dynamic is different from a Caring Unit and it requires a different type of leadership.

To illustrate, one of our young couples in a Caring Unit lost their twenty-two-month-old son to a deadly disease. Their lay pastor carried most of the pastoral ministry during Matthew's illness and difficult months following his death. Most Sunday School teachers would not carry this heavy responsibility for their people. In contrast to Sunday School teachers, lay pastors counsel and stay in close touch as well as teach the families within their Caring Units.

With our small facility it makes sense that we multiply the number of congregations, Sunday School classes and other groups. The church then operates in units and each unit requires leadership. Multiplied ministries require multiplied leadership.

We have not experienced difficulty in finding and developing new leaders. Can it possibly be that the reason many churches do not have more lay leadership is that the laity has so little opportunity to be anything more than functionaries?

One other note concerning the use of lay leaders for ministry. Once a church gains the reputation for actually using lay leaders, rather than being threatened by them, that church can expect leaders to join its ministry. Many of our leaders have, in the past, felt that they were a threat to the pastoral leadership in their churches. They were too good as teachers, counselors, evangelists, etc., and it made the professionals uneasy. We are committed to structuring around these people and freeing them to do the work the Holy Spirit has assigned them.

## Seeing the Potential of the Major Ministry with Modest Facilities

It is my hope that this book will be of help and encouragement to readers from all types of church structures. But the focus is obviously on those in city churches with facilities for 200 to 400 people. Imagine the large number of churches like yours in the city. Every time you drive by an evangelical church housed in a modest facility, imagine 1,000 or 2,000 people meeting there. See the possibilities if hundreds of people from that church were effectively ministering to the target groups of the city. What if the millions of dollars we are now spending on new mortgages, interest and maintenance of buildings were channeled into people ministries?

Those of us with modest facilities have tremendous ministry potential. Our small plants have more assets than liabilities. We can be glad we don't have more to maintain. If our people are unleashed into the city, our modest facilities will become the home base for major ministries.

When we consider unleashing the church, the facility is very important. But it is not as critical an issue as the role played by the senior pastor. If the senior pastor desires to see the church unleashed, it will likely happen. If not, it really doesn't matter much what others may try to do.

### Notes

1. Ralph Neighbour, *The Seven Last Words of the Church* (Grand Rapids: Zondervan Publishing House, 1973), p. 164.
2. Stephen Board, "The Great Evangelical Power Shift," *Eternity*, June 1979, p. 17.
3. Neighbour, *The Seven Last Words*, p. 169.

## Chapter 7

# The Senior Pastor in the Church Unleashed

I was eager to get to know my new friend. We met at a pastors' retreat. I was then a seminary student serving on the staff of a large metropolitan church; he was the senior pastor of a smaller but growing ministry. I really wanted to pick his brain; I was already looking to him as a role model. Most of my ministry experience had been in a parachurch context, and as a result I knew very few pastors personally.

He taught me a lot quickly. He was committed to the serious study and teaching of the Word. Whereas my ministry experience had been limited to young adults, he was concerned for everyone, bed babies to senior adults. He loved the people in the church and God was blessing his ministry. I welcomed the opportunity to get to know him better.

On the final day of the retreat he shared a major personal burden. His church board was pressing him to add another full-time staff person. He admitted quite openly and honestly that he didn't want to take that step. He didn't want to share "his" ministry with another pastor.

About four years later I bumped into him unexpectedly. I inquired how he had solved his problem. He didn't share any details but stated that he had moved to a smaller church which needed only one full-time pastor.

The foregoing example is in many ways not typical. Most pastors can tolerate other people on the staff full time. Not many would leave a successful pastorate for a smaller ministry. The situation *is* typical, however, in that the possessiveness of the senior pastor was a problem.

## The Senior Pastor Is the Key

The biggest obstacle to unleashing the church is not rural psyches, entrenched lay-power structures, lazy, unmotivated people or small facilities. It is the senior pastor. If you are a senior pastor you are probably sick of hearing that you are the key. Everyone who wants to implement a program in your church tells you that you are the key. I am likewise tired of hearing it, but it's still true. As I once heard a pastor say, "The pulpit is the boiler room." It is the senior pastor who sets the tone and direction of the ministry.

If you are a lay person, let me advise you not to fight the pastoral staff. Take Paul's instruction in 1 Thessalonians 5 seriously, "Now we ask you, brothers, to respect those who work hard among you, who are over you in the Lord and who admonish you. Hold them in the highest regard in love because of their work. Live in peace with each other" (vv. 12,13).

I have met many people who stayed in churches to fight the leadership. I have never found one who was successful. Don't stay and fight; go elsewhere and find leadership with whom you can carry out Paul's admonition in 1 Thessalonians 5. Find a church where you can use your energy in productive ministry rather than destructive dissension. If going elsewhere is not an option for you, then do what you can in cooperation with your pastor. As long as the issue is not heresy or sin, always remember that God has given him the responsibility of shepherding the church. If he chooses not to share the leadership of the ministry in any significant way, he is responsible for that choice. You can discuss your feelings and ideas with him and you can pray, but the Scripture never gives us permission to bring dissension into the church because of ministry mechanics and philosophy. At the same time you can be sure that if the senior pastor is not willing to actually share the ministry, the church unleashed will remain a dream. There is something woefully stifling to the ministry of the church when its people constantly get the message, "I am the pastor."

Sharing the leadership of the ministry with others does not mean that a church should not have a leader. Many writers have pointed out that even if the structure of the church is designed for co-leadership, a leader will still emerge. The late A. W. Tozer makes the point well: "Today Christianity in the Western World is what its leaders were in the recent past and is becoming what its present leaders are. The local church soon becomes like its pastor, and this is true even of those groups who do not believe in pastors. The true pastor of such a group is not hard to identify; he is usually the one who can present the strongest argument against any church having a pastor."[1] Yes, there will always be a first among equals, but the stress does not have to be on first; it can be on equal.

As was mentioned earlier, we have co-pastors in our church. At present, I have the role of first among equals. I am the oldest, have been on the church staff the longest, and have given the most direction to the overall ministry. But we do have a real co-pastor structure. By that I mean that many people in the church consider one of the other staff members as their pastor and me as his assistant. They may attend the congregations pastored by one of the other men. If they want to speak to their pastor, they naturally go to him. I am first among equals overall, but he is first among equals to many. As we add congregations in the future, we will add more genuine co-pastors to our staff.

### The Need for Plural Pastors

The New Testament church was led by a plurality of pastors. The two most prominent churches, Jerusalem and Antioch, each had several powerful preachers. James emerged as the first among equals at Jerusalem, but with the apostles in his church he certainly did not have the role of "the pastor."

Having more than one major preaching voice in the church is a sign of health. The pastor who is willing for another to have the pulpit ministry for a portion of the church is likely to share the ministry in other ways as well.

Of course there are a few pastors who simply cannot share their pulpits, even if they want to; their preaching is too unique. Can you imagine someone trying to be the co-preaching pastor with Charles Spurgeon? There are men who are so gifted that they need large auditoriums because few in their churches would ever sit regularly under another's preaching. Such preachers, however, are few and far between. Ninety-eight percent of us do not have that problem. The pulpit can be shared regularly even if one preacher is much better than another. It can be shared by those who are very good but it probably cannot be shared by the true "pulpit-master." Not many churches have a "pulpit-master." If they do, in many ways they are truly fortunate. The people in such a church can be sure that they hear the Scripture taught with unusual depth and power Sunday after Sunday. Their pastor is likely to be an influential voice across America and around the world. They will gain an appreciation for the significance of God's Word that is sadly lacking in many churches. The danger in such a case, however, is the temptation to "sit and soak" under the teaching of the "pulpit-master" rather than seeking one's own ministry. A teaching ministry that is truly effective will encourage lay people to listen to God's call and become involved in ministry themselves.

If we have multiple congregations and share the pulpit, then we must allow the preaching pastor to become essentially the senior pastor to that congregation. For example, if the 8:00 A.M. congregation wants to move its services to a ranch and baptize in a creek, that's a decision for that congregation and its particular pastor. (We always check with each other about such plans but that's more for information than for permission.) If the 8:00 A.M. congregation wants to try a different approach to children's education, that is their decision. They have to live with their decisions, so they are free to make them. This frees all of us to understand that the Lord Jesus is the Head of His Church. There is no single all-wise, all-powerful, human "big daddy" whose control extends throughout the Body. This freedom is realized within a context of discipline and structure; it is not anarchy with everyone doing what is right in his own eyes, rather liberty which comes from Christ, the Head of the Body.

## The Image of the Successful Pastor

I'll never forget a ministry field trip we took while I was in seminary. We visited a successful church and had lunch with "the pastor" and some of his staff. The pastor shared some of his earlier experiences in small struggling churches, then he warned us of problems similar to the one experienced by the pastor mentioned in the beginning of this chapter. He went on to say that if we started in small churches and God blessed us, some day we would have to put on additional staff. Not only would we have to share the affection of the people, but we would have to allow other people to carry on ministries that we would probably feel we could do better. Among the pastoral staff present at the table with us was the director of Christian education. He had written several books and was considered one of the best Christian education men in the country. The senior pastor nodded at him and said, "I know I could do a better job in Christian education, but I don't have the time." We students sort of laughed and pretended we understood him to be joking, but he wasn't. Shortly afterward, that Christian education director resigned. In fact, that church has had a continual turnover of staff; only the senior pastor seems securely in place.

The senior pastor is the key. If he is free to share the ministry, the church unleashed is likely to be the result. When I was in the military and in college I ministered within a parachurch organization. I was always encouraged by those working with me to share my ministry, to develop other leaders. This is the parachurch's philosophy of ministry. It means that a leader doesn't guide people up to a certain point and then drop them. He will help them to reach the maximum potential in their Christian walk. Often that will mean that in many areas they will excel their instructor. But this should be no threat. On the contrary, the greatest challenge a leader faces is to train others who can, from a human perspective, go on to do a better job in the ministry than he. As a senior pastor I still believe that. I have told the Lord that I will thank Him for whatever leadership He raises up in the church, even if it means they will someday replace me. I am confident He will have a place for me to minister and that's all that matters.

When we began to build a staff I asked God for men and women who would excel me. God has honored that request. Pastor Sherwin Crumley knows far more about music and education than I will ever know. It's that way in other areas throughout the staff. My co-pastors' abilities do not threaten me; they minister to me. I have admitted to the church that I am not the best at any phase of the ministry. We have better preachers, teachers, counselors, one-to-one disciplers, theologians, apologists, evangelists—you name it; and someone in the church excels me. As a result, who is the best is not an issue. The only thing that matters is the working of the Body.

A commitment to developing leadership other than yourself has a price tag attached to it. I am hesitant to share this with you because I'm really ashamed of it. Lest I sound too altruistic, let me admit that "sharing the glory" has caused me some ego problems. In a parachurch context it seemed natural, but in the church it has been more difficult than I imagined.

About a year and a half ago I found myself becoming depressed. The ministry had never been healthier but I resented even that. Since I was approaching forty, I'd like to chalk it up to that new whipping boy "mid-life crisis." I really did relate to Conway's description of himself: "I feel like a vending machine. Someone pushes a button, and out comes a sermon. Someone pushes another button, and out comes a magazine article. The family pushes buttons, and out come dollars or time-involvement. The community pushes other buttons, and I show up for meetings, sign petitions, and take stands."[2]

I realized, however, that the real issue was a basic sin problem that I had not dealt with. I thought I had settled the shared-leadership issue long ago. Yet all of a sudden I felt this tremendous need to be visibly appreciated. I knew that I was appreciated and people continually expressed their appreciation but it wasn't enough for my hungry ego. I frequently thought about those pastors who had built their ministries differently and who had received all kinds of trips and material things. I began to dwell on how good those pastors really had it.

A pastor in a shared ministry has a price to pay. Of course the things that were bothering me were a small price indeed. Nevertheless, I offer this warning to those who share their ministry and unleash their church: When the poor-little-old-me blues strike, you may wish you had done it another way.

Those feelings are now behind me. But the experience itself was not totally negative. For the first time I could really appreciate, on a feeling level, the reluctance of pastors to share their ministries. It's not that most pastors are out to get as much as they can out of people; rather it has more to do with the demands made on pastors to always be giving people. We are called on to give to others at crucial times in their lives. And it should not be surprising if we are sometimes afraid that if we share our ministries we'll lose out on the return giving most of us feel we need.

### Alternative Models of Successful Leaders

Let's think back to the pastor I mentioned at the beginning of the chapter. He didn't want to share his people's affections. We noted that he solved the problem by moving to a smaller church which is not typical. The typical way to solve this problem is to add staff personnel but to be very sure everyone knows he is only assisting the senior pastor. Most pastors who fear the competition of their associates simply build larger ministries while being careful to keep everyone in his or her place. In such churches there is normally a constant turnover in staff, while the senior pastor stays on for twenty or thirty years.

Ministries that have been built on this model are not necessarily bad. In fact, most of the great churches in America have this type of senior pastor. And that's part of the problem. We have set them up as the model of perfection for all pastors to emulate. But we need some alternative models. We need to see churches flourish under teams of pastors. If we look closely at such a team we can expect to find a pastor who is first among equals, but without an emphasis on *first*.

We need alternate models of leadership in our churches for several reasons. One major reason is the role pastoral candidates are presented by our present models. Students now usually see themselves as either low-keyed pastors of small churches or as eventually having the capacity to rise above the crowd and become "the pastor" of a large church. Few envision the possibility of being part of a genuine team of co-pastors. They anticipate joining a team of pastors' assistants rather than a team of pastors.

No wonder so many pastors are struggling. We have gone to school in a fortress environment. We have developed a fortress mentality and see ourselves as "lords of the castle." A few students with unusual ability will be able to combine the fortress mentality with the "the pastor" image to become role models for the next generation of students, while the majority will limp along in small ministries feeling generally defeated and pessimistic about the ministry potential of their church.

It's time we had an alternative model. Pastors who share all phases of the ministry, who are eager for God to raise up gifted leadership in the church, and are still being used in significant ministry can provide that alternative.

### The Senior Pastor Unleashed

The senior pastor is the key to unleashing the church. He can be the first among equals, but the stress must be on *equal*. I believe that if he is really committed to the concept of the church unleashed, he can see it happen within five years. Rufus Jones, a retired pastor and denominational leader, once shared with me that he believed any pastor could shape a church within five years if he: (1) stayed under the authority of Scripture; (2) allowed the Holy Spirit to lead; (3) loved the people; (4) developed a clear-cut strategy (in our case that is the church unleashed); (5) communicated effectively.

Notice he said within five years. When God

wants to make an oak tree, He takes 100 years; when He wants a squash He takes six weeks. He is working from the perspective of eternity. We can move toward our objectives slowly; the important thing is to keep moving.

### Notes

1. Warren W. Wiersbe, *The Best of A. W. Tozer*, (Grand Rapids: Baker Book House, 1978), p. 75.
2. Jim Conway, *Men in Mid-Life Crisis*, (Elgin, IL: David C. Cook Publishing Company, 1978), p. 57.

## Chapter 8

# Building an Unleashed Staff

Recently while sitting across the table from a pastor friend of mine at a banquet he told me of his plans to write a book on multiple-staff relationships within the church. During the conversation I mentioned to him that over the past ten years we had never had a full-time pastoral staff member leave our church. My friend responded that perhaps I should write the book he was intending to produce. While an entire book is far beyond my intentions, some thoughts on the pastoral staff in the church unleashed are in order.

### Organizing a Church Unleashed Staff

*The staff in the church unleashed needs to be free to pursue their callings within the Body.* We have often said at Bear Valley that one of the major objectives of the ministry of our church is to develop an atmosphere where everyone can be at his maximum for God. Everyone includes staff members. Pastoral staff ought not to be sacrificed on the altar of obscurity so that the "senior" pastor alone achieves his vocational zenith. Listen to this sad letter from an assistant pastor:

"I have been at Calvary Church for 19 months, and I'm seriously looking for involvement elsewhere. I'm sure I could write a book about the problems I've had here at this church—although I don't know if it would tell anything new.

"I wish seminary had prepared me for the actual priorities in a typical church regardless of what they tell you when you are hired (the Sunday morning/evening/Wednesday evening ritual, then 'fellowship,' the budget, the property, committee work, Christian education, missions, outreach—in that order for Calvary).

"I wish seminary had told me what to look for in terms of a pay package (little or no awareness or care about what it means for an individual to seek a profession in C.E. and the responsibility attendant on the church to help you make it.) I could go on. I would alter the church staff course (is it required? It should be) and call it 'Survival Tactics for Church Staff Workers' and include such topics as, ' "How to Psyche Out" a congregation in the early days,' 'How to Maintain and Build your Congregational Image,' 'How Power and Authority Function Within a Congregational Body,' and 'How to Know When to Bail Out.' I present these only somewhat tongue-in-cheek.

"A friend suggested I look to the area of Christian publishing or a college teaching slot as possible options for the immediate future. I'm ruling out further local church work because of the bad taste it has left in my wife's mouth. She has been isolated socially and drained emotionally. And as a couple, we're starved for friendship. The church has done very little to sense or meet our needs and I really have no one to support me here.

"Please understand that I am in no way embittered by my experience here. Merely disaffected and wiser. My ego has taken a beating, but I've been forced to lean harder on the Lord through it all.

"Please uphold us in prayer, and I would also appreciate any job possibilities you might steer me toward."

If job descriptions are considered necessary by a church, they ought to be left very broad allowing for the individuality of each worker. We can anticipate greater creativity from those who are free to become all God wants them to be. If this blossoming, creative leadership threatens the senior pastor the church will inevitably move toward the rigidity of a fortress mentality.

Ideally anyone in the church should be free to become the senior pastor. In some of our churches God may even desire to do what He did with Barnabas and Paul. At the beginning of their missionary journey in Acts 13 Barnabas was clearly the leader. However by the time they reached Paphos, in verse 13, the Scripture says, "Paul and his companions." God Himself simply changed the leadership. It's important to notice that Barnabas didn't leave; he kept on as part of the team. God should be able to change the leadership in our churches without the demoted ones automatically leaving.

If everyone within the Body is free to pursue his calling, the entire Body becomes responsible to discern what God is doing. There may come a time when anyone in the Body might be called to repeat the words of John the Baptist, "He must increase, and I must decrease."

*The staff in the church unleashed needs to experience a genuine shared ministry.* Most of our evangelical churches suffer greatly because of possessive pastors. Pastors often refer to the people in the church as "my people" and that mentality extends into "my ministry," "my offerings," and so on. The church unleashed cannot afford the luxury of possessiveness. We need to reaffirm the fact that the Lord Jesus is the living Head of the church and the Great Shepherd. All the rest of us share in being a part of the Body. We have no right to become possessive of His Body.

I have already discussed the beauty of a moderate facility and the need to share the preaching responsibilities in a multiple-congregational structure. But the pastors must share more than the preaching. We must share the people's loyalties. I expect people who minister in the music ministry to look to the minister of music as their "main" pastor. In our structure we have "lay" pastors leading small-group Caring Units. I would expect people in Caring Units to look to their lay pastor as their "main" pastor. It's all right if discipleship group leaders, Sunday School teachers and people with similar roles become the main pastors for those segments of the church.

It's healthy to have all kinds of main pastors in the church as long as the Head Pastor is the Lord Jesus. I'm not talking about the kind of divisions or factions that Paul describes in 1 Corinthians 1. Rather, I'm talking about the senior pastor avoiding the usurping of the role that Jesus has reserved for Himself in the church. The senior pastor must be willing to share the pastoral role with those to whom the Great Shepherd has given it.

*Look within the Body first to find staff for the*

*unleashed church.* Recently a church in our area had two of its full-time staff members resign. The church did the obvious thing—they commissioned a search committee to seek nationwide for replacements. But perhaps the obvious thing is not always the best thing. Perhaps the best place to look for staff people is within the Body itself.

The strategy of the church unleashed is to listen to the Body and to allow the Body to shape itself. It follows that if vocational leadership is needed, it's likely that the Body has already produced it. A majority of people on the vocational staff at Bear Valley were first lay people in the church. Admittedly, our location near several fine Christian schools is an advantage. But the story of how our second full-time pastor joined our staff illustrates that available students in Christian schools are not the only reason we first look within.

Sherwin Crumley was a member of our small choir when a minister of music resigned. He led the choir as a volunteer while he was vocationally in transition between being discharged from the Air Force and trying to find a teaching job. During this interim period he was doing construction work and ministering with our choir. People began responding enthusiastically to Sherwin's leadership. Although up to that time he had taken no formal training as either a pastor or a musician, it soon became obvious to us that God was putting His stamp of approval on Sherwin's ministry.

When we asked Sherwin to join our staff full time, we gave little consideration to the fact that his credentials lacked formal education in music and Christian education and that he had very limited experience. No search committee would ever have considered him for the position we awarded him. But then, as now, our first response to replacing staff or hiring new staff was to see if God had raised up new leadership evidenced by the church's response to their ministry.

Now some eight years later the choice of Sherwin for the position has been clearly shown to be the right choice. He has had a tremendously successful ministry, and over the years has picked up the formal education needed in his fields. But his primary credentials continue to be that God called him by blessing his ministry within the church.

There are several advantages in looking first within the Body for vocational staff. In the first place you know them and they know you. The normal procedure of candidating, on the other hand, is loaded with peril. People are invited in from the outside on the basis of recommendations and/or resumés. They put on their best face for the church for a weekend. The candidate is trying to find out what the church is really like. The church is trying to assess the candidate's character and skills. But the setting is usually far too superficial and the time spent together too brief to really get to know each other. It's like having a blind date and then the next day trying to decide if you should get married or not.

When you hire from within, not only do you know each other but the person the church hires has already acquired a ministry track record in that church. Someone hired from the outside, however, may have been effective in a previous church but may for some reason become ineffective in his new assigment. Effectiveness includes a lot of important issues: Does he relate well to people? Is he a hard worker? Does he sense a call from

God and understand the spiritual gifts God has given him? Does he understand those things that are unique to his field of ministry? If we know that he has these qualities we can always send him to future classes, seminars, training courses, and we can buy him books and tapes.

It's amazing that we continue to put so much emphasis on a formal education for people in vocational ministry. Educational resources are so numerous and available we can educate people on the job. We ought to be looking for ministry effectiveness and we're best able to spot them within our own churches.

*Allow the Body to determine what kind of staff the church needs.* A ministry that is run from the top down will have its set staff requirements. But a ministry that is shaped from the bottom up is never really sure what its next staff needs will be. Maybe people who leave the staff shouldn't be replaced. Maybe God has a different structure in mind or a different ministry emphasis for the Body.

If a singles pastor were to leave Bear Valley, maybe God would have that ministry led by a lay person. Perhaps instead of replacing the singles pastor, God would have us hire someone for full-time wilderness and camping ministries. The possibilities are certainly as infinite as the God directing them.

The church unleashed can't afford to take a set approach to hiring its staff. It shouldn't look for people on the basis of resumés and paper credentials. Nor should it automatically continue the normal pastoral jobs if the Body hasn't produced someone for a position that's been vacated. Maybe God wants that position dropped or left to volunteers, and new vocational staff for another job.

## Build a Home Base and a Field Staff

The church unleashed will need to look at its staff differently than the fortress church. In the fortress church the staff positions are almost standardized. But in the church unleashed, staff people for some of the target-group ministries may be needed as well.

Target-group leaders comprise what we at Bear Valley call field staff. It's important not to tie up this leadership in a lot of meetings. So we don't expect people working with international students or street people to be in the weekly staff meetings held for those working at the home base in Christian education, music, youth and similar ministries.

The field staff does not require constant close coordination with anyone else. That makes it doubly important that the field leadership be people who can be trusted to do their ministry without a lot of close supervision.

## Build a Vocational and Volunteer Staff

In today's churches we are used to working with volunteers in such ministries as Sunday School and choir. Why then should we not use volunteer leadership to lead prison ministries and outreach to unwed mothers? The key is to let volunteer leaders do the ministry God has called them to do rather than a ministry some committee or staff member has "recruited" them to do.

Churches must be willing to invest in these volunteer workers. They need to know that the church will provide the resources they need. This may include things such as training conferences and written materials. At Bear Valley we also build a leadership retreat weekend into our annual budget. We pay for a weekend at a nice Christian conference ground for volunteer leaders and their spouses. The weekend is a time of sharing what has happened in their ministry, of setting new goals and of being refreshed by the fellowship of others involved in the various target groups.

What determines whether our workers are paid or volunteer? Many of our volunteer leaders are volunteer only because (1) they can manage the ministry while working at their regular jobs or (2) their mates earn enough money so they do not need extra income.

Sometimes volunteer leaders start out under one or both of the above conditions, but things change. The church should always be ready to consider changing a volunteer ministry into a paid ministry or vice versa when conditions permit.

One of the dangers in discussing volunteer and vocational leadership is that we might fall into categorizing people in our churches. We could then become guilty of thinking in terms of the professionals, the semiprofessionals and the amateurs. That mind-set is directly contrary to the New Testament doctrine of the priesthood of every believer or to the teaching that every believer is to be equipped for ministry. Somehow the early church managed to build up recognized leadership (for example, see 1 Thess. 5:12,13) and yet was able to pursue equipping every believer for the work of the ministry. If our objective is to have everyone at maximum for God, that will mean leadership positions for some but not all. We can trust the Holy Spirit to show us whom He has called to lead our various ministries.

Leadership that has been ordained of God can be very effective when working from the home base of the local church. Such leadership needs to be held accountable but also needs to be freed up to do the ministry. In our ministry the leadership, vocational and volunteer, expects the church to approve and support its ideas for ministry. In ten years I can remember only one idea that was flatly rejected by both the staff and the board of deacons. During my first year of ministry at Bear Valley, a part-time youth director made plans to draw the attention of the entire city to our youth ministry. His plan was to have our kids stand on top of the church building and read the Bible from cover to cover over microphones, around the clock. He had visions of TV coverage, papers picking up the story and so on. But all we could see was irate neighbors trying to sleep while someone was blasting the book of Numbers over a PA system at 2 A.M.

This youth pastor was one of the first persons we hired, and from that experience we learned something. Leadership, both volunteer and vocational, must understand and be in harmony with the personality of the church. It is important to have leadership that the Body does not have to say no to. The best way to achieve that is to develop leaders from within the Body.

# Chapter 9

# Unleashing the Laity

At a Navigator conference years ago the main speaker referred to what he termed "front-line" and "rear-echelon" ministries. As a combat veteran he had vivid memories of the difference in attitude between those directly joined in battle on the front lines and those indirectly involved a few miles behind in the rear echelon.

The guys on the front lines didn't complain much. They were too busy fighting the enemy. Camaraderie was built quickly. People had to work together; it was a matter of life and death. They took their objectives and strategy seriously—successful execution was imperative. Little things, such as how good the food tasted, didn't matter significantly. What did matter was that they were still alive to eat it.

Once you went a few miles behind the front, however, attitudes changed drastically. Back there, griping was a way of life. Men complained about everything—the food, the weather, the officers. Something was wrong with everyone and everything.

The speaker used this illustration to talk about the ministry of God's people. If we are involved in front-line ministries, we will be involved in people's lives. We will be dealing with them over issues such as salvation, repentance, spiritual growth and deepening the level of fellowship with our Lord and other believers. As we share our lives, we will become involved in their vocations and families, and they in ours.

Front-line ministries happen through teaching or participation in a Sunday School class; or they may develop from a contact made through specialized ministry to a target group. Or a ministry may grow out of a friendship without the structure of any particular ministry. Whatever the context, the objective of a front-line ministry is always the same—to see another "rooted and built up in [Christ], strengthened in the faith as you were taught, and overflowing with thankfulness" (Col. 2:7).

In contrast, rear-echelon ministries are concerned primarily with planning and programming. The issues tend toward: How are we going to keep the kitchen clean? Which contractor are we going to use? How are we going to get the water fountain fixed? Which materials are we going to use in the high school Sunday School class? Then there is, of course, that ever-present question, Who can we get to take the vacant spot on our committee?

People in the midst of the battle develop the healthiest attitudes. Being in the battle isn't necessarily fun or even always desirable to the combatant, but it certainly carries more meaning than frittering away time and talent on impersonal needs.

Earlier we noted that Pastor Halverson of First Presbyterian Hollywood discovered that out of a membership of 7,000, only 365 positions were available for lay people. To fill all the slots the church program required—teaching, choirs, boards, committees, auxiliaries, etc.—took only a tiny fraction of the congregation if people held only one job. But since many talented people carry double and triple duties, most of the laity were "unemployed." But the problem is much, much bigger than idle church members. Not only are there too few positions, but too many of those available positions are likely to be rear-echelon jobs, not front-line ministries.

Is it any wonder God has raised up hundreds of parachurch organizations? He obviously wants someone on the front lines ministering to people. Actually, First Presbyterian Hollywood has far more than 365 potential positions. They, as every church, can employ their entire laity. And I mean by "employ" more than just living a good testimony where they live and work. I mean to encourage people to engage in specific ministries which ought to be the work of the church. In the Los Angeles area, for instance, they could use 365 host families for international students alone.

### A Ministering Laity Can Solve Two Problems

According to the survey taken by Larry Richards which I quoted earlier, the church's main problem is getting lay people involved in ministry. If we can solve that problem we will solve two others.

First, *we will dramatically reduce the internal "people-problems"* that seem to automatically materialize out of rear-echelon involvements. You do not usually have to know pastors very long before they begin to share that they live with a constant flow of complaining and griping. It is almost taken for granted that beneath the surface in a local church there are rumblings. The pastor's preaching isn't good enough; the nursery isn't taking proper care of the babies; the carpet is the wrong color; so-and-so deserves to sing more solos. Churches are riddled with people who have clashed over some issue in the past. In many cases there are still hurt feelings long after whatever they wrangled about has become a dead issue.

Pastors know that candidating to become the new pastor of a church can be treacherous business. You preach in the church a few times; everyone puts his best foot forward, including the candidating pastor. Then with a lot of enthusiasm you reach an agreement and the honeymoon period begins. Later, the pastor may use the phrase, "the honeymoon is over." That is usually when all the unresolved bad feelings and conflicts begin emerging.

When I visit with people who are interested in Bear Valley as a possible church home, one of the most exciting things I have to share with them is that, to my knowledge, ninety-eight percent of the time we have no "people problems." By that I mean that I am not aware of any rear-echelon griping and gossiping. Sure, there are plenty of people with problems; in fact, all of us have problems. But seldom have I heard any negative rumblings over management or programming issues.

I am convinced that our absence of petty internal problems is due to (1) numerous front-line ministries and few rear-echelon jobs and (2) the diversity that exists throughout the church.

We've already talked about the dynamics of the

front-line ministry. Most of the people in our church are so involved with other people they don't have the time or energy to put into griping sessions. Whether within the normal program of the church or in target-group ministries, our lay people are more concerned with the spiritual development of others or about an issue that has recently come to light in their own lives than they are with sniping at one another.

Diversity also plays a key role, I believe, in keeping petty internal strife to a minimum. If people don't like my preaching they can go to Pastor Thompson's congregation. If they enjoy a formal service with a choir, fine, it's available. If not, there are informal services. If they like to wear jeans to church and want a place to bring friends who live in jeans, they can choose a service that is compatible. If they feel we ought to be engaged in doing a certain ministry, we're willing to listen and work with them.

This may sound like an all-out attempt to pamper or to reproduce the chaotic situation we read about in Judges, "Everyone did as he saw fit" (21:25). That, however, is not the case. We have not digressed from orthodox theology, or biblical ethics. We have not pampered rebellious people. We have simply recognized and encouraged the diversity of the Body.

The Body has many different parts with many different needs. When I think of the immense task of ministering to all people in all stages of life, all types of professions, all levels of spiritual maturity—each person with his own unique, personal history, I am overwhelmed. No wonder the Lord designed so much flexibility into the Body. We ought to capitalize on that flexibility, allowing people the atmosphere for worship and fellowship which will most encourage their spiritual growth, and permit them to be fully used by God.

Instead, we tend to think everyone ought to be like us. If a formal worship service where everyone wears a coat and tie is best for me, I'm likely to think that it's best for everyone. If a marriage-encounter weekend revolutionized my marriage, it will revolutionize everyone's marriage. If I found the "key" to my spiritual life in a witnessing seminar, everybody will find the key there. We try to fit everyone into our experience. But God simply doesn't work that way. People need the diversity within the Body to find what is best for them, not necessarily what we're sure they need.

A ministering laity, as opposed to a functionary laity, can help our churches solve the problem of petty griping and gossip. People need to be on the front lines of ministry. They need to be involved in the lives of people in their choir, in their target group, or in their children's programs. Questions concerning water fountains and the color of the carpet need not be a matter of concern. Of course this presupposes that someone *is* responsible for rear-echelon maintenance. But these problems need not consume the attention of everyone in the church, or indeed the total attention of anyone.

A second problem a ministering laity can solve is *the elimination of our disobedience to the Great Commission.* Paul describes the ministry of the church as spiritual warfare. In Ephesians he describes the soldier armed for battle and in 2 Timothy 2:3,4 he tells Timothy to "endure hardship with us like a good soldier of Christ Jesus. No one serving as a soldier gets involved in civilian affairs—he wants to please his commanding officer." In warfare, the last command supercedes all others. Our Lord's last command was, "But you will receive power when the Holy Spirit comes on you; and you will be my witnesses in Jerusalem, and in all Judea and Samaria, and to the ends of the earth" (Acts 1:8).

The last thing He said was "Take the gospel everywhere." That's not just an idea or a suggestion, it is a command! If a church is not operating at maximum in terms of the Great Commission, it is a disobedient church. Of course only the Lord knows what the potential of any given church is; therefore He alone can judge it. But each Body should examine itself to see whether it is measuring up to our Lord's last command.

From a human perspective we can assume that if a church has someone with gifts to minister to refugees, the church is responsible to help him or her do so. If there is no structure for refugee ministry, one must be allowed to come into existence. People must be convinced that the church will build structure around the ministries that they feel God has called them to do. If the church doesn't enable that person to minister to refugees but elects them, instead, to a kitchen committee, that church is disobeying the command that supercedes all commands.

The laity in the evangelical church has enormous potential. We have the people to proclaim the gospel and make disciples in every segment of our society, and we can send thousands more overseas. In thirty years Campus Crusade has built its overseas mission force to over 11,000 and they started without a given constituency. There is a manpower potential in the churches of literally millions. If those millions are unleashed into people ministries, we will truly confront this generation with the gospel.

### Keeping People on the Front Lines

People progress in their spiritual lives when they are in front-line ministries. What can we do to get them there and keep them there?

One thing we can do is minimize the importance placed on the rear-echelon jobs of the church. True, someone does have to figure out which contractor to use and someone does have to decide what kind of vacuum cleaner the church should buy. But let's not tie people up unnecessarily with those kinds of questions.

In our case the single board of the church, the deacon board, decides about the contractor and the vacuum cleaner. That is the kind of thing deacons did in Acts 6. The New Testament church had management problems too. Grecians were complaining that Aramaic-speaking widows were being favored in the distribution of food. The whole church became preoccupied with the issue. They began acting like some modern-day Baptists who must call an all-church meeting to make a decision. But in Acts 6 they didn't have a meeting to settle the issue. Rather, they elected deacons to make management decisions so the rest of the church didn't have to be burdened with a rear-echelon issue. They didn't become a Baptist church after all!

If the church is going to concentrate on front-line ministries it must select people it can trust to do the rear-echelon management and give them the authority to do it. If we have a youth pastor, let him or her run the youth ministry. Don't saddle the leader with a structure requiring the youth ministry to be administered through a youth committee. For this committee-structure approach to ministry normally lacks high internal motivation and commitment to do a given ministry.

A person is probably a youth pastor or a lay youth leader because that is what God has called him or her to be. Chances are good that he is highly motivated. On the other hand, it is unlikely that all members of the youth committee have that same motivation. They may be on the committee because there was no one else to do it; or there was apparently nothing else they could do; or perhaps one of the committee members is a teacher and everyone has told her that she is a "natural" for the committee; or, worst of all, a member may be there just to be sure that everything is done right and no one gets away with anything.

The committee-structure insures that the unfortunate person in charge has to channel his or her ministry through a group of people who are often poorly equipped and poorly motivated to do the ministry. He encounters unnecessary criticism; everyone is cautious—the committee's job is to be skeptical; what will the rest of the church think? No wonder there are so few pastors working in the areas of youth, education and music who really keep their enthusiasm and high motivation over the years. Any good leader can find the help needed to do an effective ministry if he or she does not have an elected, standing committee obstructing the way.

### Ministry Is the Best Motivator

If people are doing what God has called them to do, then probably they are doing what they want to do. I have always appreciated Paul's insight in Philippians 2:13, "For it is God who works in you to will and to act according to his good purpose." God gives us the desire to do what He wants us to do. Of course, there are exceptions, but it is generally true.

Occasionally after a retreat or a particularly powerful service, people come away challenged to do something. Then within a week they lose it. They were merely responding to the appeals of men. It is sad to see pastors trying to motivate their people with fear, ought-to, or you'll-be-blessed motivations. God uses want-to motivation because that is the only kind of driving force which works for any length of time. Paul says it is God who works in us. The Holy Spirit working within directs us where He wants us to go and He often uses want-to motivation to do so.

Lasting motivation comes from within. And nothing motivates from within like being involved in a front-line ministry to which God has called us. Recently I spent two hours with a couple who have been ministering to refugees for over four years. The first two years Chet and Carol conducted a fruitful ministry with the Hmong people from Laos. Among those gentle people they found many Christians and some who spoke English well. Then they felt the Lord leading them away from that established success to work with Cambodians. The Cambodians were a different story. They spoke little English and knew virtually nothing about Christianity. Compared to their work with the Cambodians, their ministry to the Hmong had been fun, exciting and easy.

Still they felt God had called them to the Cambodians and, in doing so, He supplied the desire to stay in a difficult ministry. For a year they went to an apartment complex to study the Bible in English with two Cambodian men. They became good friends with the men and several other Cambodians in the complex. After a year of these studies they met a Chinese seminary student; Wai-Kwong Sun was God's provision; the Cambodians are ethnic Chinese and Wai-Kwong spoke their dialect. Since Wai-Kwong Sun's involvement in the ministry, things have changed. One week the two Cambodians study English; on the alternate week they study the Bible in Chinese. Wai-Kwong will be leaving to do further graduate work in Germany but he is confident that these two men will become Christians in the near future. These men are well respected in the Cambodian community and if they come to know Christ it will open tremendous possibilities among the most difficult of the refugee groups.

How does a pastor persuade lay people such as Chet and Carol to carry on a four-year work with refugees? The pastor doesn't; the Holy Spirit does. This ministry goes on without committees or fanfare. It continues because of a desire to be obedient to God's call. We are confident that God will give our people the deep desire to do whatever ministry He wants them to do. There are many ministries in which we are not involved; God has not yet given anyone in the Body the call and desire for them.

One such ministry is to the cults. I had never thought about target-grouping the cults until a young couple in the church heard God's call to invest their lives in ministering to people entangled in their snares. As we talked about the possibilities, I began to see the enormous potential of their work. We talked about a clearinghouse of information on the cults. We could recommend specific books and tapes to people with particular questions. We could compile a list of addresses of people who had been converted to Christ out of the cults so we could ask them to help us with similar converts. Whenever a cult was gathering in Denver we could send out people with appropriate tracts to witness to them. Then, we could find out where the cult members lived and systematically go door to door to witness to them. The ministry could teach frequent classes on the cults within the church (since many cult members come out of Baptist backgrounds). The ideas flowed and we were soon excited about reaching the cults. Then, before the ministry could get started, the couple moved. We would still like to see the cult ministry become a reality but we've learned to practice "relaxed concern." When God is ready He will give someone else the want-to to specialize in a ministry to the cults. Once they have God's call and He has given them a desire to serve, we won't have to worry about the program. The ministry will get done because the leadership already has that inner motivation. Perhaps the couple interested in the cults will hear God's call to begin such a ministry in their new church. But will their new church encourage or even permit such a ministry?

At Bear Valley all we need to seriously consider starting a new ministry is someone to say that he or she wants to do it. But we simply don't start ministries if God has not supplied the motivation. I am not aware of anyone in the church serving the Lord because "someone has to do it." If a person is confident that his want-to has come from the Lord, he or she can depend on everything he or she needs flowing from this motivation. Without the assurance that it is God who wants us doing a ministry, we can't count on anything. Will we have a Vacation Bible School next year? Only if someone has a desire to direct it.

As in any other organization, Bear Valley staff members are expected to carry on certain staff responsibilities. But even here we don't draw up a job description then insist that the person fit that mold. Rather, we shape the responsibilities around that person's specific call and abilities. We also give staff the freedom to do the ministry the way which will work best for them.

## Preparing Leadership: The Built-in Fallacy

Have you ever stopped to think about the built-in fallacy in the way we prepare people for leadership in churches? As students they go to school in a fortress environment. For years they spend much of their time in classrooms and libraries. The assumption is that if they hear the lectures and read the books they will be equipped to be leaders in the church. The reward system is built on grades; students live and die for grades.

After several years of this they are asked to take a position in a church. Functionally, the church bears little resemblance to the school. The school-trained leader assumes that the way you equip people to live the Christian life is to give them a lot of facts about the Christian faith. You can't test the people, but you can surely lecture them. So we lecture in Sunday School, in the worship service, in the evening service, on Wednesday evening and in all kinds of seminars and workshops. If dumping content on people produced mature Christians, the church in the United States would be by far the most mature church which history has ever seen.

No wonder the frustration level is so high among those coming out of school to serve in the church. In school they tend to listen and study or they could not pass the tests. In school, interest level in the subjects was usually high; students were studying with the impetus of a vocational motivation. But in the church not everyone is interested when you announce a study of some area of theology. Furthermore, in the church no one cares what grades you made in school. Grades go from being all-important to not counting at all. One of the first things I tell students in my classes at Western Bible College and Denver Seminary is that no one has ever asked me what grades I made in school. People really don't care.

The world in which students prepare for church leadership and the world in which they serve have little resemblance to each other. The parachurch organizations, on the other hand, usually look to ministry to prepare people for their staffs. What do the Navigators want to know about a potential staff member? Can this person lead people to Christ and disciple them? Does his or her lay ministry demonstrate that this is a reproducing Christian with several generations of believers to prove it? The parachurch organizations prepare people for leadership primarily through ministry. No wonder the parachurch organizations are running away with the ball game when it comes to effective ministry.

This is not a suggestion that the churches stop looking to Christian colleges and seminaries for help in training leaders. After years of training with a parachurch ministry I desperately needed the kind of education I received in seminary. I needed the hours of classwork, library research and the discipline of preparing papers and writing tests. There is nothing wrong with what the schools are doing; it is just that we expect too much of them. Most are simply not in a position to provide the practical ministry training needed.

Perhaps this means we ought to expect much more of the local church in preparing candidates for leadership. These future leaders should be people with proven ministry ability. Education ought to supplement their ministries, not vice versa. If people receive primary training for the ministry in a "fortress" school setting, is it little wonder if they bring that fortress mentality to the church? A ministering laity who stays on the front lines, however, will require leaders who think, pray, plan and stay on the front lines themselves.

Isn't it ironic that the churches' biggest problem is getting the laity involved in meaningful ministry, while the culture's biggest need is the very gospel and value system our laity have? The need for the local church to focus on front-line people ministries is urgent. When we major on ministry we solve the host of internal problems that normally plague a church as well as fulfill the Great Commission.

If we are to expect more local church involvement which, in turn, will prepare people for vocational ministry, we must set about providing more opportunity to minister. Hence it is the church unleashed that should become the primary training ground for the next generation of church leaders. One of the often repeated statements we have heard from students at Bear Valley is, "I came to Denver to attend seminary, but I now see that at least half of my training has been my ministry involvement here in the church."

# Part II

# The Methodology

The focus of this book so far has been entirely on the *strategy* of the church unleashed. I have not stressed a particular methodology because I see the greatest need in our churches as not primarily methodology, but rather more thoroughly thought-through strategies. In fact, concentrating on methods would do more harm than good. In his helpful book on renewal, *Love, Acceptance and Forgiveness*, Jerry Cook begins a chapter on strategy by saying, "One thing working all kinds of devastation in the life of the church is the failure of the leadership to have a solid philosophy—a well-defined concept of how a church ought to operate and why."[1] A chapter on methodology then could possibly fuel a current fad or tempt someone to subscribe to a concept of church life handed down ready-made.

Therefore, before going on to the need for ideas on methodology, we should first consider some of the dangers involved.

## The Danger of Methods Without Strategy

We are living in the age of the franchise. We are used to seeing near-identical motels, department stores and restaurants. Everywhere we go the same familiar golden arches tower upward, chubby boys hold up platters of food and sleepy bears carry candles to bed. And although this franchise method may have worked well for American business, I don't believe God ever intended it for the church.

It's easy to see how some churches are distracted by faddish organizational mechanics. After all, when we observe a ministry we usually see the methods while the strategy behind them remains invisible. Therefore we attribute the success of what we see—the methods—and overlook the guiding, invisible principles.

A healthy church does not depend on methodology. The dynamic is Spirit-filled people meeting other people's needs in Jesus' name, wherever they are. You can't reduce that to methodology. Concentrating on practices instead of principles is like building our houses on sand. When the storms of doubt, criticism and failure come, we immediately begin looking for new methods.

Before a church spends much time on methodology it should spend a lot of time on philosophy of ministry. Ron Oertli, worldwide coordinator of the Navigator 2:7 discipleship course for churches, speaks with hundreds of pastors from all types of denominational backgrounds. More than once he has said to me, "Frank, pastors and churches desperately need a strategy for church life and growth. Most pastors think primarily in terms of methods rather than strategy and it's frustrating them to tears."

## The Danger of Insensitivity to Situations

While principles may be universal, practices certainly are not. Inevitably methodology carries with it the message, "This worked for us, so it will obviously work for you," but to quote an old Gershwin musical, "It ain't necessarily so." Each local church is unique. Many approaches that work in other churches won't work for you, and vice versa.

The church unleashed should have a natural feel to it. We have occasionally tried programs that worked great elsewhere but in our particular situation seemed forced and unnatural. We found we had to be sensitive to our church's history, the type of people attracted to it, the size and mentality of our city—in short, the unique personality of our church.

We also needed to be sensitive to the fact that our church has some unique possibilities. If we had merely concentrated on systems other people were using, we might have overlooked ministry methods emerging from within our own body.

## The Danger of Stunting the Growth

There is something very valuable about feeling God wants you to do something but you don't yet have the foggiest idea of how to go about it. There is something necessary about making mistakes and experiencing failure.

We have recently learned that lesson in a fresh way. Several years ago part of the strategy we mapped out was to begin planting mission churches as soon as Bear Valley reached a thousand active members. This number was chosen so we could plant the new church with a healthy number of people while still leaving the mother church sound.

After reaching our membership goal, we started a new congregation which we hoped would become our first mission church. We added a lay person to our staff to pastor the new group and asked all those interested in this first mission church to begin meeting as a body for Sunday worship. The idea was to incubate this embryo church within Bear Valley facilities until it was ready to move out on its own.

In the meantime an existing church in our city invited one of our pastors to candidate for them. We encouraged him to do so and, if he received their appointment, to take as many people with him as he could to this new church. So despite our carefully laid plans, our first mission didn't turn out to be a plant at all, but rather the sharing of our people with an already existing body.

We have since disbanded the mission congregation and, more importantly, we have learned some things. We learned that we need to expand our thinking beyond mission churches to existing churches. We also learned that it's difficult to "create" a new congregation and bring a new person on staff to pastor it even though he already is a member of the church.

We now see the need to groom pastors for the future by having them preach regularly in the various congregations of existing churches. The next time we ask people to join a mission congregation, their pastor will have already established solid bonds of rapport and credibility. Again, it's the principle of unleashing people who have a proven track record.

Fortunately, our church is used to change. The fact that our methods didn't work the first time didn't devastate us. Why? Because we're still pursuing the same strategy. Consequently, this process of trial, failure and redirection has been very valuable to us. As we work through these processes that unleash the church we are forced to keep our eyes focused on the living Lord and not on some "How to Do It" manual.

Despite these dangers, there is still a valid need for discussing methods. Without some ideas on methodology a book such as this could lead to a lot of frustration. To say that reaching international students is a crucial foreign missions opportunity, and can become a part of any church in a college town, is a good start. But some helpful ideas on how to go about starting and maintaining such a ministry has a variety of benefits.

### The Need to Prime the Pump

The book of Proverbs reminds us that "iron sharpens iron" (27:17). Ideas stimulate ideas—at least that's the theory behind this methodology section. Many churches have a great deal of experience at thinking about the methodology within the fortress. But most have probably never considered a specialized ministry to a target group such as international students or street people. The obvious initial questions are: Where do we start? What are some of the problems we can anticipate? How do we make contact?

With these basics in mind I sent a questionnaire to the leaders of several of our target-group ministries asking them the following. In your ministry:

1. What facilities are needed?
2. What type of staff is needed?
3. What are the financial implications for the church?
4. How does your ministry tie back into the local church?

5. What are the most important lessons you have learned so far?

6. What are some of the future possibilities? The people responding to these questions had anywhere from six years to six months experience in their target groups. The results of these questionnaires form the essence of the following chapters.

### The Need to Share Workable Ideas

Sometimes ideas that work in one church ministry won't work in another; sometimes, of course, they will. Many of Bear Valley's ministries grew out of our becoming aware of what other churches or parachurch groups were doing.

For example, if you work with street people you are working with people who are normally employed only enough to get by. Almost any kind of "handout" will attract those whose life's aim is mere survival. What can a ministry do to avoid becoming a welfare ministry to street people? How does a work program fit into sharing the gospel? These and many other such questions must be answered if a street ministry is to succeed. If we are aware of possible pitfalls inherent in working with our target group, we may save months, even years of needless frustration.

If a church considers working with international students it should first acquire certain basic information. It should, for instance, become acquainted with International Students, Inc. This parachurch organization has for years specialized in ministry to foreign students and so has accumulated tremendous amounts of information on various cultures and how to witness to people of different faiths. Churches planning to minister to internationals should also be aware that most major campuses have foreign student advisors. Who are they? What do they do? Would-be ministers ought to know that bypassing them sometimes leads to serious problems for ministering to their students.

The attempt in this book to say something about the methodology of the church unleashed will only scratch the surface, at best. I was reminded of that recently when a lady who is interested in ministering to those in prison visited the church. When one of our pastors visited her, she sent him away with a large stack of materials about prison ministries. Included in these was a 318-page book entitled *A Christian's Guide to Effective Jail and Prison Ministry*. The point is, each of the ministries mentioned in this section could have an entire book written about it if we tried covering all the bases. Covering all the bases however is not the intention here. Our purpose is merely to prime the pump, to sharpen iron with iron.

Perhaps we can begin to see a network of churches across the country working in target-group ministries, sharing the ideas that have worked well for them.

**Note**

1. Jerry Cook, *Love, Acceptance and Forgiveness* (Ventura, CA: Regal Books, 1979), p. 23.

## Chapter 10

# How to Break the Stranglehold of Counseling

As I was finishing my eighth year of pastoring at Bear Valley I was in bad shape. The ministry was everything I ever dreamed it would be, but it had also become some things I hadn't anticipated. For example, I had never projected spending 15 to 20 hours a week in counseling, nor had I foreseen crisis situations tying up my time, emotions and energy for days in a row.

By the time I finally figured out what was happening, I wanted to leave the pastorate. As I look back now at that period, it's easy to see that the pressure most bogging me down was the heavy counseling load I was carrying.

I have always had great respect for the ministry of counseling. Some recent studies have shown that twenty-one percent of the people seeking counseling go to psychologists, twenty-nine percent to psychiatrists, and forty-two percent go to their pastor. In spite of the explosion of the counseling professions, many still want to talk to someone in the church about the problems they are having.

In the 1950s the statistics above may not have meant a lot in raw numbers. But today, with the immense problems we're experiencing from the breakdown of the family, pastors are swamped with people who are seeking counsel. During the 1960s the fabric of this nation came apart. I left the United States to serve with the military in Germany in 1959; I returned in 1963. After having grown up during the tranquil, puritanical fifties I couldn't believe I was returning to the same country. Not only were there bars featuring nude dancers, but I had to drive through National Guard checkpoints to get to work. When I entered college in Southern California I heard language I never expected to hear in public. The four-letter words weren't confined to the free speech areas either. They were used liberally in classrooms by students and teachers alike.

Perhaps one event in my college life sums up the ferment and chaos of the sixties more than anything else. I was taking a final in an art course. About one-half hour into the test, when everyone was thoroughly immersed in the subject, a young lady in a revealing knit see-through dress stood up and started cursing the teacher. She screamed that the test was too hard and that it was totally irrelevant. The teacher was shocked; but before she could respond, another girl attacked the one who was screaming at the teacher. They began wrestling in the aisle. Soon a few more wrestling matches broke out, then a man entered the room dressed in a black robe complete with hood. He carried a crucifix and began going up to each student and blessing them with the sign of the cross. This started a whole parade of characters. Someone came through passing out strawberries. Then a clown-like performer came into the room with a juggling act. All the time there was fighting, the screaming of profanities, people being blessed, others either enjoying the strawberries or throwing them around the room. It was literally mind-boggling. It was not at all what I had expected the atmosphere of the final exam to be.

But then I realized it was intended to be mind-boggling. It was a staged "happening" designed to communicate the existential message of the sixties. The world is chaos. Things you think are important—like finals, grades, decency and order—are meaningless.

Needless to say, the teacher, who knew nothing about this planned event, was stunned. She finally put an end to it when someone shut the lights off, wheeled in a movie projector and flashed a pornographic movie on the classroom wall.

I have thought about that experience often. It happened in 1967, the height of the turbulent sixties. America was a different place than the one I had grown up in during the fifties.

Of course, not all the results of the sixties were negative. But one result we had better be prepared for in our churches is that people are more confused than ever about the basic issues of life. Is abortion right? How long should I stick out this marriage? Do husbands and wives have God-given roles? How can I raise my children as a single parent? Can I be a committed Christian and a homosexual? There probably aren't any new questions; it's just that so many more people are asking the old ones.

The point of all this is simply that counseling loads in our churches are strangling thousands of pastors who ought to be freed up for other things.

A few years ago I heard a student ask Dr. W. A. Criswell, pastor of the famous First Baptist Church in Dallas, Texas, about his role as a counselor. He took on a pained expression and said, "You know, counseling is like taking a dipper to the ocean. You can spend all your time dipping with all your might, and when you are finished you haven't made much of a dent." Maybe that's too pessimistic. Maybe we can make some significant dents. But I'm convinced the vast majority of pastors shouldn't be dipping in the ocean of counseling.

## Counseling and the New Pastor

Jerry Cook describes the situation of a new pastor in this way: "Our church was at one time very small. I sat around in my office reading and looking busy and hoping something would happen."[1] That's the way it usually is when one begins a new ministry, especially if the church is small. People don't come to the pastor with their problems right away, and he often wishes they would. He has time to do some counseling; he wants to get to know people. He knows people are having problems and he wishes they would trust him well enough to share them with him.

As the counseling load grows, the pastor's sense of acceptance and self-worth grows with it. The counseling is also helping him in his personal growth. He is having to deal with tough issues under fire. He may not feel that it's his obligation as a pastor-counselor to give a steady stream of pat answers, but he can't help but wrestle with each situation for his own life.

The counseling ministry is also helping his preaching. It helps get a pulse on the people. He is less likely to preach like an ivory-tower saint if he is living with hurting people during the week. Of course now he's faced with the delicate question, "Can I say what I intended to say about this subject in light of the fact that so-and-so has shared he has this exact problem?" But in general the counseling helps his preaching.

In most growing ministries, however, within a few years the counseling ministry reaches a point of diminishing returns.

One of the reasons we had been able to do as much ministry at Bear Valley as we had was that our leadership wasn't tied up in a committee-oriented bureaucracy. But we soon learned that the hours we were saving by not attending committee meetings were being spent in counseling. Of course we might say, "Counseling is people ministry, and that's what the staff ought to be doing." While it's true that counseling had us involved with people, it is also true that it usually focused on problems. The squeaking wheels were getting all the grease. And a lot of non-squeaking, potentially very productive people were not getting the grease they needed to do their ministries well. For every hour we spent talking about a personal problem in someone's life, we could have spent that hour planning a strategy on how to open a new ministry or do an old one better.

So eight years into the pastorate I was exhausted. I had promised the church I would spend twelve to fifteen hours a week preparing my sermons. I intended to speak only once a week, but I wanted that to be a rich and spiritually beneficial time for the congregation. Now I was counseling fifteen hours a week, and often it was nonscheduled crisis ministry. I no longer had time to spend with the leadership of our ministries. New ministries were opening, old ministries needed encouragement and I couldn't get to the front lines. I was wiped out.

At that point a very fortunate thing happened. I had been too buried in the problem to figure a way out so God provided one for me. He did so through a woman who was counseling professionally with an organization called Life Management Inc. She did not have an advanced degree in counseling, but she had been developing her counseling skills for the past several years. Since her husband made enough money to support the family, she offered to resign her paid counseling position and do my counseling for me on a volunteer basis.

I realize now that if God had not provided a capable volunteer we should have hired a counselor for our staff. I encourage any pastor who envisions leading an unleashed church to plan to phase out of counseling fairly early in his ministry. The pastors we had hired to do Christian education, music, youth and preaching should have been free to major on the productive people in their ministries. Recently I asked Jan, our counselor, how many appointments she had. She said she had sixteen and some of her trainers had ten. Those twenty-six counseling sessions are not being neglected, but they have been diverted away from our staff.

## Unleashing the Counseling Potential of our Laity

Counseling in today's church is a big job. In one sense I'm glad it is. I'm glad people are still turning to the church when they are hurting. And the church must take seriously its responsibility in the area of counseling. What can we do to free our pastors to major on the people who are productive in the ministry and still not ignore those who need help in counseling?

*Step one—a designated staff counselor.* The church unleashed, somewhere in its development, needs a designated staff counselor. Perhaps there is someone in the Body whom the church could invest in by providing counseling courses to help improve skills. Maybe there is a counseling professional that the church could hire even if it is only part time. Maybe there are students in a counseling program in a local Christian school that could be phased onto the staff. Or, best of all, a competent, available volunteer such as the Lord provided for us.

A church can expect serious problems if its pastor is committed to equipping laity for ministry but retains his role as the primary counselor in the church. There will soon be three groups who will be looking to him for guidance and encouragement. The first group will be leaders deeply involved in one of the many ministries going on in the church. They need the pastor's encouragement, and it's important they feel they can spend time with him. A second group will be new people coming into the church. They will be needing some direction, some encouragement to develop and use their spiritual gifts. A third group will be those who for one reason or another are hurting badly. They need to talk to someone, someone who cares, who will pray with them and help them see what can be done to start a healing process.

The pastor or pastors will be singled out by all three groups. The third group will get the immediate attention because they are hurting. The others can wait, at least we think they can. As the church grows and its reputation for helping hurting people grows, the third group is likely to increase dramatically. People in the church refer friends and family members. The out-of-town calls from people concerned about someone in our city increase. Soon the pastoral staff is loaded with counseling sessions, unless it has learned to divert the counseling ministry to a single designated person on the staff.

*Step two—develop a peer counseling program.* The designated staff-counselor shouldn't be expected to do all the counseling. Often he or she should refer people who prove to be too complex to other trained professionals. A good list of referral counselors is a must.

Equally important, however, is the development of lay people in the congregation to help with the counseling ministry. It has been encouraging to see a growing emphasis on peer counseling. Gary Collins' book *You Can Be a People Helper* is a much needed word.

The laity in our evangelical churches are logical choices for counseling as they have the Holy Spirit living in them and are often serious students of Scripture. God has equipped many with spiritual gifts and natural talents that enable them to be effective in helping people in counseling situations.

Soon after Jan took over my counseling responsibilities, I encouraged her to begin developing a peer counseling program. Another church nearby, Faith Presbyterian in Aurora, Colorado already was running such a program. In my typical fashion (I'm not very creative, but I copy very well) I told her to look at their program. They were very helpful and their designated counselor gave us the following advice:

1. Inform the church that a peer counseling ministry is starting; all interested should meet at a certain time and place.

2. Have a prepared training program that can be explained at the first meeting. At Bear Valley we use six, two-hour sessions for the course we have designed. In addition we hold monthly meetings designed as a support group for our peer counselors and to further develop their skills.

3. Explain that counselors are to fill out reports on their meetings with counselees and these reports are turned in to the staff counselor.

4. Develop a network of referrals and assure peer counselors that they're not expected to work with people who need professional care.

5. Encourage people to take the counseling training even if they have no plans to do any peer counseling. The principles learned in the training will enrich their marriages, jobs and relationships in general.

In addition to this advice that we began with, we have learned that the peer counseling ministry has some built-in pitfalls.

To avoid the pitfall of gossip, strict confidentiality is insisted upon. However, the counselors should be told that everything shared may be discussed with the program director at the peer counselor's discretion.

Then there will always be people who want to do peer counseling who for some reason should not. It should be stressed that even though the training has been completed, it's the director's decision on whether clients should be assigned to the peer counselor. If there is a person you don't plan on using he should be told so and, if possible, why.

*Step three—change the pastor's image.* I have found it helpful to have it known in the church that I don't do extended counseling. I do encourage people who want to talk to me about a counseling problem to make an appointment to see me. But they need to know I will see them only one time; after that I will refer them on to a professional outside the church or to Jan.

Taking the "I-will-see-you-for-an-initial-session" stance accomplishes at least three things. First, it makes me available to the entire church, the hurting and the healthy. I never have to say, "No, I won't see you." Second, it keeps me in touch with some of the individual hurts of the church. And third, it lets the productive, healthy people know I'm available.

One of the things that surprised me when I first entered the pastorate was that people felt they had to have a problem in order to talk to me. It seemed that all I heard was, "Pastor, I don't know what to do." Or they often talked to me about someone else's problem, "Pastor, my poor sister in Chicago . . ." I wanted to get up in the pulpit and say, "It's OK to talk to me about something other than a problem."

But now our people realize that I'm not loaded down with counseling. They see me as someone available to talk to about things other than problems.

### The Peer Counseling Program

The evangelical church's dependence on "the pastor" has hurt us in a multitude of ways. Particularly treacherous, however, is the tendency to look to the pastor as the church's primary counselor.

As we enlist lay people to do a ministry of peer counseling we can anticipate a number of benefits to the church.

More people will be given an opportunity to exercise their spiritual gifts and natural talents by having opportunities to counsel. Therefore, more people will receive quality counseling. When I was carrying a heavy load of counseling and doing a hundred other things in the ministry I found I couldn't give much thought to each individual situation. But a peer counselor who has just one client can really concentrate on and pray for that situation.

Another benefit is that the pastoral staff responsible for leading various ministries will have more time to invest in their ministry leadership. The ministry life span of many vocational pastors will be extended simply because they will not be burned out trying to empty the oceans with a dipper.

My heart aches for my pastor friends who are being eaten alive by counseling. They have so many potentially productive people in their churches who need their time and encouragement. The pastor also needs to be refreshed by working with these productive people. Only by directing most of the ministry of counseling away from the pastoral staff can the leadership remain productive and the church be unleashed.

Following is a resource list of some of the materials we have found helpful in training peer counselors.

1. Lawrence J. Crabb, Jr. *Basic Principles of Biblical Counseling*. Grand Rapids: Zondervan Publishing House.
2. _____ *Christians Become Capable Counselors*. Grand Rapids: Zondervan Publishing House. A model for helping caring Christians become capable counselors.
3. Gary R. Collins, Ph.D. *Christian Counseling*. Waco, TX: Word Books.
4. Gerard Egan. *The Skilled Helper*. Monterey,

CA: Brooks/Cole Publishing Co. A model for systematic helping and interpersonal relating.

5. Taylor-Johnson Temperament Analysis Test, Psychological Publications, Inc., 5300 Hollywood Blvd., Los Angeles, CA 90027.

6. H. Norman Wright. *Training Christians to Counsel*. Denver, CO: Christian Marriage Enrichment. A resource curriculum manual.

7. _____ Premarital counseling materials developed by Norm Wright and Christian Marriage Enrichment. Family Counseling & Enrichment, 1913 E. 17th St., Suite 118, Santa Ana, CA 92701.

**Note**

1. Jerry Cook, *Love, Acceptance and Forgiveness* (Ventura, CA: Regal Books, 1979), p. 67.

## Chapter 11

# Ministering to Singles

A "Death and Dying" seminar seemed an appropriate place to meet a nurse from the intensive care unit. She had been divorced for two years and, like so many things she did, she was attending the seminar alone. Although our group consisted of three married couples she still felt drawn to us. We soon learned that the second day of the conference was her birthday, so we had an impromptu party.

As we got to know Lynn we found out that she really wasn't involved in a church. Since her divorce she felt she no longer fit in. Fortunately we had started a special target-group ministry to singles. That meant we had a ministry we really felt good about inviting her to. A year later Lynn invited those same three couples into her home to celebrate the anniversary of our discovering one another's friendship. During that time she had become deeply involved in our singles ministry. She had experienced significant healing of the hurt of the divorce. She also met a man her age who had never been married, fell in love, and married him. Together they remained in the singles ministry as group sponsors. Since then Lynn and Jerry have had a lasting impact on scores of people. The Bible studies they have led and personal relationships they have developed have been beneficial to many.

What happened to Lynn probably couldn't have happened without a "singles" ministry. And I don't mean a college and career Sunday School class. By singles I mean people generally 25 years of age and above who have never married or are single again—either through divorce or a spouse's death.

While singles ministries are much more common in evangelical churches than they have ever been before, they are still the exception rather than the rule. I'm told that more than one-third of the adults in our cities are single. In a city like Denver the figure runs into the hundreds of thousands. The day has arrived when the church in the city with a special singles ministry ought to be the rule rather than the exception.

The first thing any ministry needs is leadership. The church can encourage this leadership to emerge if the desire to start a singles ministry is well known and if the pastoral staff keeps the challenge of singles before the Body. Then when the time is right, God will provide.

It's important to allow the singles themselves to shape the ministry. Our singles leadership has suggested that a church encourage an initial task force to brainstorm the possibilities. Some of the issues likely to be dealt with will be:

1. What's the best place to meet?

2. If we meet in a restaurant can we coordinate a nursery at the church?

3. What might be some strategic places to advertise?

4. What will appeal to non-Christian singles?

5. Are we going to have any age guidelines for the ministry?

It's important to go ahead and start the ministry even though many of the questions still do not have firm answers. For once the Lord has provided leaders and a handful of interested people, we must not procrastinate.

### Type of Leadership Needed

Leadership throughout the church is critical. Singles ministries are no different. Following are some of the characteristics we have looked for.

*Leadership that is positive.* In the midst of a group of people, many who are divorced, trying to raise children alone, mourning a broken engagement or the death of a spouse, it's easy to feed on the negative. It's important that leaders steer the group toward a positive outlook. For example, in our singles breakfasts we noticed that when our people introduced visitors they often seemed to highlight the negative. "This is Patty Johnson, she has been divorced a year, she just lost her job, she needs a place to live and her car stopped running this week. Patty really needs our prayers." We found we had to instruct people to be positive when introducing people. That goes for the tone of the group in general. It doesn't have to be rah-rah or phony or out of touch with the harsh realities of life but it does need to be positive.

*Leadership that is relationally oriented.* It's important that the singles teacher be capable of handling the Scripture. Personally I believe everyone who teaches with regularity ought to have studied systematic theology. There are several good studies in serious theology geared for lay people.

It is also important, however, that the teacher not conform to the academic mold that believes the way to teach is to dump content on people. The teaching in a singles class needs to be consistently practical in handling relationships.

For the recently divorced or widowed person the handling of relationships is now often a huge problem. What about reentering the world of dating? How should a divorced woman handle her married girlfriend who now sees the divorcee as a threat? Or what about the "swinging single" image at the office?

Sometimes there are relationships where the issue is assertiveness. How is a single female to be sure she gets a fair deal at the garage or from the TV repairman?

Then there are the sensitive family relationships. How are we as Christians to relate to our former spouses. How about our families or former in-laws?

A teacher in a singles ministry must have a good grasp of Scripture and of theology. But the teaching dare not be academic in tone; it needs to be practical in the area of relationships.

*Leadership as fellow strugglers.* This does not mean that the best leadership for singles classes ought to be single. In fact couples are normally better. What it does mean is that leaders ought not to be looked upon as people with all the answers. It's normally best to avoid giving advice. Singles will often want you to play the role of their former spouse in telling them what to do. That's the time to resist giving answers and help them think through the options themselves.

It's also key that leaders be fellow strugglers in

the sense of being nonjudgmental. If singles are struggling with their consciences, the Holy Spirit, not the leader, should be the convicting one. This doesn't mean that we refrain from teaching the Christian view of marriage and divorce or sex. It doesn't mean we convey the idea of cheap grace. Rather, while we teach these truths, we do so in the spirit that Jesus exemplified when the woman who was taken in adultery was brought to Him. He told her two important things: (1) He didn't condemn her, and (2) she was to go and sin no more.

*Leadership that has realistic expectations of people.* The singles leadership will likely experience less commitment in this group than they would working with married couples. In the city large numbers of singles will move through a group looking for the "best deal." Unfortunately the best deal is often one that "offers me the most with the smallest return on my part." Therefore when a social is planned, there is often a widespread attitude of, "I'll be there if nothing better comes up." As a singles ministry develops, however, leaders should expect several high-level-commitment small groups to emerge. But when dealing with the overall group, if it's dynamic, changing and large at all, expect a sizable fickle contingent.

*Leadership that has the ability to live with change.* Singles are extremely mobile. They may move into and out of the group quickly—some because they have been dating someone in the group and have then broken up; and others, many times the most committed leaders, because they get married and move on to a couples class. Throughout the church, change is the name of the game. But it's more accelerated in a singles ministry than anywhere else.

*Leadership that has an ability to counsel.* Much of the counseling in a singles ministry will be informal. Since singles do not have spouses to turn to, they often turn to the group leader for advice. While it's normally best to avoid giving advice it is still a great opportunity to teach practical Christianity by helping someone discern the real issue from a Christian viewpoint. If a singles ministry grows large at all, perhaps over thirty or forty people, it would be wise to develop a peer counseling ministry in the church. In our experience large numbers of singles have taken the peer counseling training. Many are interested in the course content for their own lives, but others become peer counselors to those in the singles group seeking counseling.

*Leadership that is not easily discouraged.* A large portion of singles have been divorced, in our ministries sixty to seventy percent.

Even though divorce is much more prevalent today, it's not any less painful. It remains one of the most agonizing of human experiences, and many divorced people need years to recover.

In dealing with these hurting people the leadership often has to take what I call a ten-year step of faith. That is, they have to see the potential of a person and then realize it may be a very long, slow process before he achieves that potential. In fact, there will be a lot of times when there doesn't seem to be any movement at all. During these lulls, leaders must not let discouragement defeat them, and they also must not give in to some form of "easy solutionism." It's easy to send someone off to a seminar or give him or her a book to read that (if they will only listen) will solve all their problems. It seldom does, however, and a singles leader may be tempted to think there is no hope for this person.

I realize that I may have painted a lofty picture of the type leadership needed for singles. We can be confident, however, that God will supply the Body with leaders whom He has equipped.

## Activities

Generally singles groups are more active than couples classes. There are all kinds of obvious possible activities. Let me mention just a couple of principles which our singles leaders have found important.

First, singles leadership can easily get into a "monkey on your back" situation if singles have the idea that leaders are responsible to plan their social lives. Recently a single fellow wanted the group to sponsor a rafting trip. The trip cost $25, which to him was no problem. When he came to the leadership with the idea, they said fine, you plan it. In the process he found that the trip would take an entire day, making it difficult for those with small children; that they would have to travel a long way into the mountains; that the cost of $25 did not include getting there and back; and so on. All these factors led to a low response from the singles and a canceled trip.

It was much better that the guy with the idea tried to put it together rather than putting the responsibility on someone else's back and complaining when the event failed to happen.

Second, small groups and special training sessions are helpful. There seems to be a consistent need for various types of training sessions. Assertiveness training has been offered on a regular basis and the response has been good. Single-parenting sessions and money management are the basis of some of the other singles small groups.

In addition to these life-situation type sessions,

there needs to be the small group designed to help people grow in their spiritual lives. Bible studies, prayer groups, small groups built around a common ministry are continually forming, dying out and re-forming. These groups are especially important to us since our Sunday morning breakfasts are designed to reach the unchurched single. Therefore the content on Sunday morning is often not enough spiritual food for the growing Christian.

### Dangers

*Singles groups may withdraw from church.* A few years ago I heard of a church in our city that started a singles ministry similar to the ministry at Bear Valley. One difference was they used some high-powered advertising which generated several hundred singles quickly. In time that ministry separated from the church and became an independent organization.

One of the dangers of any specialized ministry is that it might break away from the main body and go it alone. Avoiding this calls for a creative tension to be maintained between the specialized ministry to the singles and the structure pointing the single to involvement with the rest of the church.

If the singles are meeting in a building separate from the church, it will require extra effort to integrate them into the church family. Our staff is encouraged to be contintually looking for singles to teach Sunday School, help with choirs, become youth sponsors, get involved in small groups that have both married and single people in them.

We do not want our singles ministry to offer another singles world, as do singles apartment complexes and singles bars. Rather, when singles come to Bear Valley we want to have a ministry that recognizes their special needs but at the same time also discourages their committing themselves solely to the singles group. They are not to be an exclusive club. Their commitment must include the entire body from bed babies to senior citizens.

*Beware of wolves in sheep's clothing.* Every singles group in a large city will have both men and women visit who are looking primarily for their next bed partner. While this isn't as likely to be as prevalent in Christian groups, it won't be totally absent either. These people usually are not very subtle about their desires, and they pass through a group and move on fairly quickly. They are more of a nuisance than a real threat to a group.

The type of person who *is* a real threat, however, is the person who knows the Christian vocabulary, who appears to be very spiritual, and yet has the same agenda as the people mentioned above.

About six months after I became a singles pastor a young lady called me in tears. She had lost her virginity by being involved with one of the single male leaders. In fact the guy was the spiritual leader of the group. She insisted that both of them come and talk to me. I thought they would be repentant and eager to attempt to restore a healthy, Christian dating relationship. When I met this couple I was shocked—shocked first of all because the guy was furious. According to him, their activities were none of my business. But that was just the beginning. He then launched into a defense of their physical relationship. In a nutshell, his conclusion was that for them premarital sex was OK.

I discovered this fellow had fed a similar line to other girls in the group. One of the major things that led to his being successful in taking several girls to bed (besides his good looks and having plenty of money) was his position of leadership in the class.

Since that time I've seen the wolves in sheep's clothing come and go. A few years ago there was a student from a Christian school. He walked through the door pushing his way into leadership. He eagerly offered his counsel to women who needed a male perspective. I confess I wasn't surprised when a single girl who asked him for some counseling shared they had been involved sexually several times.

These wolves in sheep's clothing (which, by the way, can be females too) are far more dangerous than the person merely passing through looking for a bed partner. Because the wolves look and sound so good, they are likely to cause far more damage.

*Sex outside of marriage is a crucial issue.* From a Christian perspective perhaps the most difficult issue for singles is sex outside of marriage. According to Scripture this area is an absolute; despite what the wolves in sheep's clothing may say, it is never right.

Obviously when you're dealing with a group of singles, and most of them do not have the gift of abstinence that Jesus mentioned in Matthew 19:11,12, you have a serious problem on your hands.

The three mistakes that a singles ministry can easily make when it comes to sex is to either (1) pretend it's not a problem and everyone is really too spiritual to be interested in sex anyway, or (2) do as our culture has done since the sixties and become too preoccupied with sex, or worst of all (3) ignoring the biblical absolutes, accept the humanist standards of meaningful, caring relationships being the prerequisite for sex.

To combat this, it's important that a singles ministry provide some appropriate times for people to share their struggles in this area. Some things may be appropriately shared in mixed groups; many things need to be shared in either a small men's or women's group.

*Learn to prevent a "dating game" atmosphere.* When I talk to someone who has recently been widowed or divorced and I suggest they visit one of the singles breakfasts, they will often say, "I'm not ready for that yet." What they usually mean is that they are not ready to join a dating club.

Once again we're faced with an important tension. On the one hand a singles group shouldn't discourage dating. On the other, dating should never become the central purpose of the group.

To overcome the latter we have found it best to discourage "pairing off" at our singles functions. Even couples who are dating rarely sit together at the Sunday morning breakfast. I'm not talking about making up a set of dating rules but rather of encouraging singles who are dating, and even married couples in the group as sponsors, to keep the couples thing low-key since it is a singles group.

*Avoid the message that marriage is the only acceptable way to live.* Most single adults think of their situation as temporary. They see themselves in a premarital state that will end when the right person comes along. And for many that's accurate. Therefore, we have always preferred married couples to direct our singles ministries. Married couples can serve as healthy models, something many singles have rarely seen. And yet this subtle modeling for marriage needs to go on amid an overall climate that downplays marriage as the only acceptable way to live. Today more and more singles are less likely to marry, or they will marry much later in life. Biblical models such as Jesus and Paul can be pointed to as an encouragement for those remaining single. The advantages of the single life that Paul states in 1 Corinthians 7 need to be seriously taught.

## Conclusion

No target-group ministry holds more potential for the church today than does this one. Singles make up one-third of America's adult population; they are in our cities by the hundreds of thousands. We have found a special ministry to them has greatly helped our Christian singles grow spiritually and become fully integrated into the church. We have also found that non-Christian singles tend to be responsive to a ministry that is not out to exploit them. The evangelical church has the greatest product in the world to attract today's single—we have the gospel. Our challenge is to find a way to bring together the ministry of the church and the wandering single.

## Chapter 12

# Foreign Missions at Home: International Students

It was our monthly senior citizen luncheon at the church. I had just met several first-time visitors when I found a vacant seat next to an "old-timer" whom I hadn't seen in months. I was looking forward to an interesting conversation, but I came away from the luncheon with more than just a conversation.

She told me how she had wanted to use her home to minister to someone. Living alone, she had plenty of space. The Lord had led her to check out the church's Friendship International ministry, an outreach to international students studying in our area. Out of this inquiry a young Indonesian girl named Justina, a Christian, had come to live with Alice.

Alice was excited as she shared a brief letter she'd just received from Justina's parents.

Dear Madame,
First of all, may we express our sincere

gratitude for having given our daughter, named Justina, the opportunity of staying with you in one house which we have never expected before.

Praise the Lord. This is a great blessing for us. We are sure that this will help her much in adjusting herself to the way of life and culture more rapidly in the States. Because this is not an easy matter.

Consequently we should appreciate you if we may entrust her to your entire care. So, please, treat her as your own child. In this way we are quite confident Justina will enjoy a nice education and getting mature in her spiritual life as well.

To end our short letter we hope that God's blessings may always be with all of you.

Justina's parents are now planning to send their other daughter to the U.S. to study and live with Alice. On top of that, they have invited Alice to visit them in Indonesia, an invitation she plans to accept.

This is only one of literally hundreds of beautiful things that happen when a church focuses on internationals. The ideas in this chapter come from Bob and Julia Wright, who have been on our church staff ministering to internationals for almost five years.

Because of the widespread separation of the local church from the academic world of universities and colleges there is a real cultural gap to be overcome before the gospel of Christ can be communicated and understood by an international student. But the resources for this type of outreach can be found in the spiritual lives and gifts of almost any local body of believers.

Many towns and cities in the U.S. have at least one college and larger cities may have several private and state colleges and universities. Many of these institutions have significant groups from Europe, South America, Southeast Asia and the Middle East. It is common for a student population of 10,000 to include from 500 to 1,000 students from perhaps fifty different countries studying engineering, business, English or the sciences. Most of these students attend school for four or five years. Those who extend their stay to acquire master's or doctor's degrees will remain for seven or eight years.

Most of these international students would like to get to know Americans better and experience our family life, friendship and hospitality. But the sad fact remains that many will return home without ever doing these things. What picture of America, what impressions of life and culture in the U.S. will they take home with them? A large percentage of them have no clear idea of Christ and His salvation. We can make sure that they have an accurate understanding of the Christian message and a positive experience of American family life.

### The Target Group

There are at least 300,000 foreign students in almost 3,000 colleges and universities in the United States today, and the number is increasing rapidly as more and more developing countries send their best and brightest young people to learn our business methods, science and technology. During their stay they will have an opportunity to learn Marxism, humanism, and moral relativism. But very few will have any opportunity to learn what biblical Christianity is. There are 3,000 such students in the metropolitan area of Denver alone. This pattern is repeated in hundreds of cities across America.

Western business and technology are seen as the key to the future and the competition for the chance to study in the West is very intense in most developing countries. Few students from these countries can afford to come on their own resources; most depend on scholarships from their governments. Others can study only through the continual sacrifice of their families at home. This intense competition means that the international student is usually very intelligent, hardworking, dedicated, competitive and goal-oriented. In addition, he or she may be competent in two or three languages. Christians here have an amazing opportunity to show these foreign guests the best America has to offer; we can send them back to their families and friends with real enthusiasm and warmth for America. More important, we can give them the truth of the gospel and help them to understand Christian values.

Frequently, the international student is from the middle or upper classes of a country where the gap between rich and poor, the privileged and the powerless, is very great. The likelihood that such a student would ever be contacted by Christian missions in his or her own country is so small as to be almost negligible. Missionaries are not usually able to effectively contact the upper levels of society in such a country, even if they are allowed entrance. Again, the opportunity for friendship and witness to these students is a gift from God, His provision for countries or classes closed to the gospel. A student who has studied in the U.S. (or any other industrialized country) can usually return to a position of leadership, power and influence. Many will gain political positions from which they can influence the direction of their country. Examples abound of ill-treated students who returned home to become powerful political figures dedicated to hatred of America.

Fortunately, examples of a positive nature are also plentiful, such as one young man from a country completely hostile to Christianity. Christians there were not even allowed schools in which to educate their children. While studying here, however, he was befriended and loved by a vibrant Christian family. Eventually, he became minister of education in his country. He not only stopped discrimination toward Christian children in the state schools but also encouraged the Christians to run their own schools and enroll non-Christian children. He had seen Christian values and principles. He understood, as he had not before, that Christianity could be a powerful influence for good in his homeland. As far as we know, he himself is not a believer.

Almost any country you can think of is represented here today by its young people, its future leaders. Some of them, contacted by Christians taking a special interest in their welfare, will return with a knowledge of the gospel. What better world view could they take back home than one based on the revelation of Christ? This represents a challenging missionary potential for any local church. Dr. Mark Hanna of Biola College calls it "The Great Blind Spot in Missions Today."

## Problems and Perspectives

A certain level of competence in English is required by U.S. colleges. Students in English language schools have special needs that the local church can meet. We can meet these newcomers just hours (or minutes) after their arrival. Friends made at this very difficult time will remain friends throughout a busy college career. For many, English study will continue after the college classes have begun. The best way for these students to improve their English is to spend time with—or better, to live with—an American family. Many students are eager for such families.

Most foreign students live in college dormitories or nearby apartments and remain isolated from normal American life. Their sphere of experience is governed entirely by the academic atmosphere and relieved only by whatever activities may occupy their vacations. Less wealthy students often cannot afford to leave town even during the summer. Isolated from home and from any sense of family, they become lonely and discontented with their experiences here. They return home with the impression that Americans are selfish and superficial.

Hospitality to the stranger is an important virtue in their homeland, and the lack of it here is conspicuous. They believe that no one knows or cares that they exist. As a consequence of loneliness and the desire for friends the student may be drawn to drugs and dubious entertainments which, especially in the Middle East countries, are not so easily available at home. Away from family and any stabilizing influences, many internationals get into trouble. A strange culture often gives the wrong signals to someone not used to that kind of "freedom." If they had trustworthy American friends this would be less likely.

Muslim students believe that America is a Christian nation. Their country is Islamic; America is Christian. Would you like to have Christianity judged according to the larger American culture of today?

"Christians can do anything they want. You (Christians) have no moral standards or rules. You don't care for others. You are concerned only with making money or having a good time." Remarks like these are frequently heard from the students disillusioned with America and with the Christianity they think they see here. Unless we seek them out they will most likely never meet a true Christian at all.

## The Church's Responsibility

Before the church was able to "go" into all the world in obedience to the Great Commission of Matthew 28, God brought the world to the church. Some fourteen national groups and languages were present at Pentecost (see Acts 2:9-12), and churches grew up wherever the new converts returned after this great feast. God is again doing in our time what He did then. He is bringing the nations to hear the gospel. The world is truly on our doorstep. The majority of those countries that will not admit Christian missionaries send their best young people into our neighborhoods. You cannot get into most Muslim countries to preach the gospel, but you can reach thousands of Muslims in Denver, Berkeley, New York, Houston or any other city with a large university. Those of us with an interest in missions overseas should ask ourselves whether God has not kept us home to participate in foreign missions in our own living rooms and at our own meal tables.

One could easily collect texts from the Old Testament to show how God is concerned for the "stranger" in the land (see Exod. 22:21; 23:9,12; Lev. 19:34; 23:22; 24:22; Deut. 10:18,19). Hospitality is not an optional extra in the Christian life; it is a *command*, a basic characteristic of the real believer (see 1 Tim. 3:2; 5:10; Heb. 13:2).

It costs many thousands of dollars to train, equip and support an American missionary in a foreign land. What better missionary to send abroad than one whose target country is his or her own home? He or she will have no language problems, will already understand the details and pitfalls of the culture and will readily be accepted as a legitimate member of his or her society. These returning Christian students do not have to adjust to a new climate or culture. They can get good jobs and take their place in their home communities. Of course, Christians returning from countries hostile to the gospel will have a trying time. But they will have the prayer support and friendship of brothers and sisters in Christ in America. They will be living proof of the international quality of the gospel. And our own awareness of the trans-cultural reality of Christianity will be sharpened through praying for the growth and witness of our friends in many lands.

### Overview of Friendship International

In developing a local church outreach to internationals, both short-term and long-range goals need to be defined and implemented. In beginning our ministry, we had three immediate needs:

Our first goal, and the goal of any new ministry to international students, was to *begin contacting students and learning about them*. We wanted to make observations about the students we would be reaching, learning from the students themselves about their backgrounds, problems and needs in this country. We began to understand the particular needs that students from a certain country or language would have.

Those interested in such a ministry should

consider the numerous possibilities for contacting internationals in the local schools. An international student ministry may already be functioning in your area. If so, you may want to join forces with that group. Certainly, you will want to meet with the leaders and be sure that you are not duplicating their efforts or competing.

If your area has a Christian college or seminary with foreign students enrolled, you can arrange to meet these Christians by going to the campus or by giving a dinner for them. Your team coordinators can then enlist their help in meeting internationals on the secular campuses. These Christian students can be an important resource for the local church ministry. They can perhaps make contacts more easily with students from their home countries. Also, they will have much to teach the team about what it means to be a student in a foreign country. They can supply accurate information about conditions in their homeland as well as suggestions about the best way to approach internationals. We should not forget, however, that these Christian students are foreigners themselves and also need our friendship and help. They too will have special problems and concerns.

The second immediate goal is to *contact the foreign student advisor on each college campus.* The advisor is responsible for helping internationals with the problems of academics, of visas and immigration, and of settling successfully into the community. For this reason he or she is wary of high-pressure groups, including over-zealous church ministries that try to influence students. It is essential then that your team establish a relationship with the foreign student advisor before contacting any international on that campus.

While advisors resist propaganda peddlers,

they are usually more than delighted when Americans (Christian as well as non-Christian) display a genuine concern for their students. The advisor needs such people to host internationals during their student years, and the prospect of a readily available supply of families is welcome news. It is absolutely vital, then, that the advisor know your team coordinators well and trust them personally to provide the help and services which students need.

It is best to be introduced to this official by a Christian faculty member if possible. In this way the advisor recognizes you as a legitimate group already known to someone on the faculty. Personal introductions are always best for smoothing the path toward practical cooperation.

In the absence of a personal introduction, your coordinators should make an appointment with the foreign student advisor. During this appointment the coordinator should define the goals of your group, outlining your plans for involvement with the college's internationals. A written proposal or outline would be useful to the advisor for future reference.

The coordinators should ask the advisor how their team can best help him or her. The advisor has a list of all foreign students in his or her college. Once the advisor trusts your team to be concerned with the welfare of internationals he or she will be glad to pass along the names of students who have indicated a wish to meet Americans. Sometimes the advisor will even supply the entire list of international students. When the names have been obtained, a personal contact can be made and an invitation given to a planned social event or to a dinner at someone's home.

Another effective way of meeting students is

through the local staff of International Students Inc. ISI has been ministering to international students for more than twenty-five years. If there is no ISI staff in your area, you can still obtain help and guidance from their headquarters in Colorado Springs, Colorado. They are willing to offer suggestions and guidelines for ministry to internationals, and they have available many helpful publications as well. A local church can request an ISI representative to give a presentation about the needs of internationals and the best methods for reaching them for Christ.

Other organizations such as Campus Crusade, Inter-Varsity and the Baptist Student Union of the Southern Baptist denomination also often have local international student programs. Care should be taken not to merely duplicate what is already being done or draw off students from one group to another. Any sense of competition between groups is unseemly and unnecessary. There are plenty of students whose needs are not being adequately met.

The third immediate goal of ministering to internationals is to *recruit volunteers from within your local church who want to become friends of internationals.* You need to assess not only who is available and willing but also what each person or family could contribute and the amount of time they are willing to give. Some may want interaction with a student once a week or less; others may want a student to live with them as part of their family. There may be those who cannot make a commitment to individual students but who wish to help incoming students on registration days or help with the logistics of hospitality dinners, or supply food or transport to take students to outings such as skiing trips or picnics.

## Ways to Meet Students

A variety of ways for meeting students must be developed to cover the needs of differing Americans as well as the varied interests and needs of students. Following are just a sampling of possibilities; others will suggest themselves as you progress in the ministry.

1. Small dinners for two or three students in the home of a volunteer who has invited another couple to meet them.

2. Large dinners for perhaps fifty or more held in a church hall with a slide show presentation on the state or with a visiting speaker talking on a topic of special interest.

3. Special parties that help to explain certain Christian holidays. Christmas and Easter are of special interest to internationals, even those who do not celebrate these holidays in their home countries. This is an ideal time to present the gospel message in a nonthreatening way.

4. Discussion groups on various topics such as world religions, distinctives of Christianity, questions of philosophy and human problems. Interest in certain topics can be determined beforehand and announced at one of the hospitality dinners. It is always best to begin the relationship with an act of hospitality and friendship before any effort is made to introduce the subject of faith or a presentation of the gospel. Each contact should build on the previous one.

5. Picnics or excursions into the countryside to see tourist attractions, or tours of the city. City tours are especially helpful for new arrivals.

6. Parties at which students prepare their own special dishes from home and serve them to their American guests, together with folk dancing or crafts. Students who have enjoyed much hospital-

ity from their Christian friends will appreciate this opportunity of reciprocating.

There are many ways of meeting international students. These students come in all nationalities, languages and religions. All of them come hoping to make friends during their stay here. Too few of them have any opportunity to do this. They are our guests and it is our God-given responsibility to welcome them and make them feel at home. We have the injunction to "practice hospitality" and to "teach all nations." With the international student we have the opportunity and the responsibility to do both.

## Chapter 13

# A Senior Adult Ministry Comes of Age

In the senior ministry at Bear Valley we work with people over sixty years of age. And this is the only blanket statement we can make about them. For aside from sharing a certain span of years they are as individual and varied as the rest of God's creation. It is of prime importance, therefore, that those who consider working with older people be ready to lay aside stereotypic views and begin to learn about seniors from older people themselves. Visit in their homes. Talk to them. If possible, seniors should participate in the leadership of the ministry from the beginning. Conversely, if mostly seniors make up your ministry team, be sure to include some younger people as well in leadership positions. We have found this intergenerational blend necessary for effective ministry.

We can, however, make some general statements about working with seniors while admitting at the same time that they are just that. But what we say is not necessarily true of all seniors.

## Who Are the Seniors?

You will probably find senior adults in two basic groups—younger seniors who are active and full of vitality, and older seniors who are less mobile and may be declining in health or mental acuity. These two groups are vastly different from one another and have differing needs. They should not be lumped into the same mold.

## Where Are the Seniors?

We have found large concentrations of seniors in four major areas:

First, *older established neighborhoods*. Senior married couples tend to stay as long as possible in the private residence they have known for so long. Some widows and widowers also remain in these familiar surroundings. Perhaps a survey conducted from house to house in these older neighborhoods would be helpful in meeting otherwise invisible seniors and learning their needs. Care should be taken to use such a survey for genuine information and not as a screen for high-pressure evangelism.

Second, *low-rent, high-rise apartments*. Most of these seniors live alone as widows, widowers or singles and come from middle-class backgrounds. The establishments where they live usually prohibit door-to-door soliciting, but may be willing to display posters about your ministry on apartment bulletin boards. It would be wise to first contact each building manager to explore what is acceptable and unacceptable in a particular building and to indicate that you plan to observe the rules. This should prevent future misunderstandings. Building a relationship of trust with managers and residents is an important step in beginning a ministry to seniors in high-rise apartments.

Once you establish contact with one resident, you are then free to call on her or him. The resident can also invite friends to the apartment for informal get-togethers and, if they desire them, for Bible studies. Many of these seniors will already have a church of their own. Others, however, will not and will gladly respond to the Body which displays genuine love and concern for them.

Third, *the gray ghetto—seniors living in substandard housing in the inner city*. Most of these seniors also live alone. Many come from lower-class backgrounds. Problems here are abundant—from the lack of basic necessities such as food and heat, to the high incidence of crime, to the human barriers of culture and language. At Bear Valley we are only now beginning to reach out to this group. Some of our workers will receive volunteer training from Denver Social Services and will go on to work one-on-one with inner-city seniors. After they have gained some knowledge and practical experience in getting to know these particular seniors (and this may take as long as a year) the workers will then transmit what they have learned to others and, we hope, begin a more extensive ministry. Currently, Bear Valley is planning to establish an inner-city church which we might be able to use as a base of operations. If this should not materialize we would seek out another inner-city church that might be willing to let us use their facilities. Or we might check into the possibilities of using community halls, the YMCA, or whatever.

Fourth, *nursing homes—establishments for those seniors who for physical or mental reasons can no longer care for themselves*. Only about five percent of seniors fit this description.

Most nursing home administrators welcome visitors and are open to Bible studies and church services on the home premises. They are also usually willing for their more able-bodied patients to attend outside activities. The more debilitated seniors will not be permitted to leave, but you should be able to minister to them in their rooms.

### Are There Physical or Mental Limitations?

People who have little contact with seniors sometimes think that all older people are frail or are in wheelchairs or are fast approaching senility. On the contrary, most older people are physically and mentally sound, possessing greater stamina than people half their age. At Bear Valley, for instance, there are seniors who travel, teach, bowl, fish, lecture, do crafts, "grandparent," write, design clothing, and serve in various ministries. Many still have their own transportation and minister by helping other seniors who do not.

But just as there are some young people who suffer from debilitating illnesses, so also do some seniors. And because of this, a ministry team should have some expert advice. Perhaps a nurse or doctor in the church or a worker from a nearby nursing home can teach your team such things as the best way to lift a wheelchair patient into a car, the most effective means for working with the blind or the deaf, and the nutritional needs of the elderly. Each of your team members should have a working knowledge of CPR (cardiopulmonary resuscitation) and the Heimlich Maneuver (to prevent fatality due to choking). Medical personnel or firemen are often glad to teach these lifesaving techniques. Local Red Cross first-aid courses might also be of benefit.

After learning these basics, two more issues need to be considered. The first is transportation. Some seniors who are in wheelchairs because of frailty or who have the use of their upper bodies can still usually ride in private cars. Those who are more seriously handicapped, however, cannot leave their wheelchairs at all and will need to ride in a van or bus equipped with a wheelchair lift. Since these usually cost several thousand dollars, you may need to borrow or rent such a vehicle from someone in your town who already owns one. Also check with local transit systems that sometimes operate buses for the handicapped.

The second consideration is building design. Examine the church building or other meeting place where those with disabilities will be gathering. Is there at least one entrance accessible to those in wheelchairs? Are doorways into rooms and restrooms wide enough? Are there safety bars in restrooms?

Sometimes minor changes can overcome otherwise serious problems. For example, can you reserve the front row of pews in your church for those who are hard of hearing? Can you provide large-print Bibles or hymnals or page magnifiers for those who no longer see as well as they once did? Other relatively simple and inexpensive aids will probably come to mind as you become more and more acquainted with the seniors in your ministry. You might also wish to contact your local associations for the blind, the deaf and the handicapped for further help.

## What Spiritual Needs Do Seniors Have?

The answer to this question, of course, is the same as with any other age group, namely: (1) to accept the gospel, (2) to grow in the faith and (3) to serve others. An effective senior ministry should be concerned with all these aspects of the Christian life. Following is a short description of Bear

Valley's overall senior ministry as it relates to these five points.

*Turning seniors to the gospel.* Once a month, ministry workers provide a free luncheon, open to all seniors who wish to come. Visitors are recognized. They receive a nourishing meal and hear advice on practical issues such as good nutrition, telephone aids available for the hard of hearing, etc., along with special music and a short devotional. No invitation is given except to return to the luncheon or to attend Sunday School and church. This open, unpressured meeting is usually nonthreatening to the unchurched and gives them time to find out what Christianity and Christians are all about.

During the next few weeks our senior-adult pastor and other workers contact those who visited the luncheon, getting to know them better and ascertaining their needs. This is a slow and gentle process. It is important that Christians not adopt the tactics of con artists who so frequently prey on older people.

Then, through personal visits or attending church and Sunday School, some seniors come to believe in Christ as their Saviour. The last step of this belief is in acknowledging what has happened to them, to possess assurance that they truly have eternal life. Many of the seniors we have met lack this assurance which is so necessary before true growth can begin.

*Growing in the faith.* Through Sunday School, church and local Bible studies seniors hear the entire truth of the Word as it relates to all facets of life. In the fellowship of other Christians they see that life modeled in practical ways.

*Serving others.* In time, seniors should begin to see areas where they too can serve, from the nursery of the church on up and beyond the church, out into the neighborhoods where they live and even "to the ends of the earth."

### What Staff Is Needed?

At Bear Valley we have a paid, part-time pastor who teaches senior adult Sunday School and supplies the pastoral gifts of concern and guidance to the senior flock. Volunteer workers are responsible for individual areas of the ministry such as outreach, transportation, education and health, public relations, activities—and in connection with the luncheon, menu planning, kitchen assignments, programming, decorations, birthdays and nursery (for workers' children). Since our monthly meeting covers such a broad range of issues we have found it necessary for one of our workers to serve as a recording secretary, keeping a written account of the meeting's business. Lastly, one of the workers (or a husband-wife team) serves as the ministry coordinator(s) tying together loose ends, trying to let each part of the ministry body know what the other parts are doing and (along with the senior-adult pastor) conducting the monthly workers' meetings.

It is important that those in the most critical leadership positions be patient, loving people and that they have some amount of spiritual and emotional maturity. Equally important is that each worker see himself or herself, not in some messianic image of "helping all those poor old people," but as receivers from older people as well as givers, and as sharers together in the new life of Christ.

**Chapter 14**

# Targeting Street People

The sleepy little town where I grew up in North Dakota was pretty static. There was, however, one mobile element that I would see on the streets of New Rockford during the summertime—the railroad bum. The Great Northern Railway had a division point in my hometown and during the forties and fifties that meant a lot of hobos would come through. Some would usually spend a few days or weeks hanging around town.

I remember talking to many of these men as they passed the time of day sitting on the bench in front of my father's restaurant. Occasionally they would do odd jobs for Dad in return for a meal or a few dollars.

## Street People Are a Fascinating, Devious Subculture

These railroad bums became my first contact with "street people." Then one summer while I was still in high school I traveled with a carnival and there I met another type of street person. During the 1960s I occasionally found myself driving down Sunset Strip in Los Angeles. Inevitably the strip was full of young people, many of whom lived on the street. Between my childhood days in North Dakota and my college days in California I became acquainted with a wide range of street people.

In the street one finds the older person, usually a middle-class dropout, often hooked on alcohol. There is also the younger crowd which tends to be much more into drugs and illicit sex. The homosexual element in the street has also grown dramatically since the 1960s. Broadly speaking, "street people" refers to those who are transient and preoccupied with just getting by. These may be Indians coming off the reservations, teenage dropouts, criminals, girls working as prostitutes, or those who are not only unemployed but uninterested in being employed.

In the street, the name of the game is survival. These people are not building portfolios loaded with assets for the future. They live a very "now" life-style. Forget about yesterday and don't worry about tomorrow. If they have been in the street any length of time they have often polluted their minds and their bodies. (It's difficult to minister to people whose minds have been fried by drugs.) Street people often come out of disastrous home situations. Many don't have any idea who their fathers are and some don't know either of their parents. Girls on the street often come from incestuous situations at home.

Street people are usually non-achievers according to middle-class values. They ordinarily have never been successful in the traditional ways— graduating from school, competing on sports teams, writing for the school paper, etc. The one thing they are successful at is getting by. That may mean heterosexual or homosexual prostitution, selling drugs, stealing, working at brief jobs or finding a handout somewhere. The means usually don't matter when the end is survival.

### Street People Have Some Things to Teach Middle-Class Christians

Despite all the problems I have just mentioned concerning people on the street, they do have some things to teach us middle-class types.

First, *we can learn something from them about living in the present.* We need not take living in the "now" to the extreme most of them do, but we do need to take Jesus' words in Matthew 6:28-34 seriously: "And why do you worry about clothes? See how the lilies of the field grow. They do not labor or spin. Yet I tell you that not even Solomon in all his splendor was dressed like one of these. If that is how God clothes the grass of the field, which is here today and tomorrow is thrown into the fire, will he not much more clothe you, O you of little faith? So do not worry, saying, 'What shall we eat?' or 'What shall we drink?' or 'What shall we wear?' For the pagans run after all these things, and your heavenly Father knows that you need them. But seek first his kingdom and his righteousness, and all these things will be given to you as well. Therefore do not worry about tomorrow, for tomorrow will worry about itself. Each day has enough trouble of its own."

In the second place, and closely related to the first, *they can teach us to come at life less materialistically.* Isn't it interesting that Jesus ties these two points together? "Therefore I tell you, do not worry about your life, what you will eat or drink; or about your body, what you will wear. Is not life more important than food, and the body more important than clothes? Look at the birds of the air; they do not sow or reap or store away in barns, and yet your heavenly Father feeds them. Are you not much more valuable than they? Who of you by worrying can add a single hour to his life?" (Matt. 6:25-27).

The street culture, with all its faults, is much more oriented toward people and less toward things than we are in the middle class. Maybe they can help us become less preoccupied with bank accounts, bigger houses and newer cars.

Third, *the street culture has a tremendous potential to produce New Testament life-styles.* We'll not find them living behind high-walled privacy fences or isolated as they drive their cars around town. In our ministry street people are the ones most eager to live in community. The life-style of Christian street people more closely resembles what we see in Jesus and His disciples than any other group. Their nonmaterialistic orientation gives them tremendous discipleship potential. They simply don't struggle with Jesus' warning "you cannot serve God and money" like we do among the middle class.

This third positive factor is born out by the response of street people to highly-committed cults. Many of the cults in this country are feasting on a street subculture that wants more than middle-class values can offer.

### Working with Street People Is a Difficult Ministry

More than any other target group we have worked with, the street ministry needs vocational staff. To be successful in this ministry you must be where the people are for huge amounts of time.

But we have found that staff persons need not have a street background. The person who has no background in drugs, crime, and loose sexual behavior is likely to do better leading a street ministry than someone who has to battle all or any of these things from their background. The people in this ministry must also be willing to live in situations that are often dangerous. And if having their material possessions stolen bothers them too much, they are probably in the wrong ministry.

In the street one often works with the victims of those sins that devastate self-images. As a result of these poor self-images, many street people develop engrained destructive habits. They often feed on failure. We have worked with people for years, have seen them reach what looked like possible permanent victory over some destructive sin only to see them lose the victory completely. Street people can often be lazy, angry, ungrateful, uncouth, undisciplined, unprincipled, and arrogant. They are often not an easy bunch to share life with. Yet I can't help but believe that if Jesus were on earth today one of the first groups He would target would be street people.

## Some Ideas on Structuring a Ministry to Street People

The street ministry needs a base of operations. Our base has been a big house where up to thirty people live in a community at a time. Presently we rent a storefront and run a coffee house, Jesus on Main Street, in the target area. This has given us a second base from which to work. These bases of operation are helpful, but ideally we feel we need more. Our strategy at this point is to eventually:

1. Run a crash pad for people fresh off the street.

2. Run a discipleship house for singles who have graduated from the crash-pad ministry.

3. Run a discipleship house for couples who have graduated from the crash-pad ministry or gotten married while at the discipleship house for singles.

4. Run a coffee house in the target area.

5. Start a church in the target area.

We have a long way to go to have a full street ministry but we can share some things that have worked for us so far.

## Running a House for Street People

We hired a young couple who had a desire to work with street people in the context of the local church. The fact that they wanted to work with a local church is important since one finds a great deal of "Jesus yes, the church no" in the street. We then rented a big house with room for our street pastor and his wife to live with a potential community of thirty. Our street pastor went into the target area to rap with people about Jesus. He invited them home to share a meal and stay overnight. Soon a core group was living in the house and they began to work at janitorial accounts to finance the ministry.

They continue to invite people off the street to the house. The newcomer can stay for up to three days without a lot of expectations. If they stay longer they join those who are in the streets witnessing (even if they are not Christians they still go along) and they also go on the work crews. The schedule of the house goes like this:

| | |
|---|---|
| 8:30 Breakfast | 12:00-2:00 Lunch and Free Time |
| 9:00 Bible Study | 2:00-4:30 Downtown Witnessing |

| 10:00 Chores | 5:00 | Dinner |
|---|---|---|
| 11:00 Quiet Time | 6:30-10:00 | Work Crews |

The janitorial accounts prove to be far more important than just providing financing. They teach one of the lessons most needed on the street, the discipline of work. Many parachurch groups have discovered that one of the best places to disciple someone is on the job. For many living at the house, this is their first long-term job, the first time they have ever provided for themselves via honest work. It is terribly important that a street ministry not become a welfare situation. That would only reinforce one of the major problems already in these people's lives.

The street ministry calls for the most rigid structure, not only in the daily schedule but also in male-female relationships. As you can imagine, the whole sexual issue is extremely volatile in the kind of home we operate. Andy Cannon, our street pastor, had run similar houses in the past. Andy, along with those living in the houses, came up with some dating guidelines. Everyone who comes to live in our street house is given the following information on dating:

### DATING GUIDELINES

Because of the unbelievable increase in divorce rate, abortion and children being reared in single parent situations, we feel that a strict view of Christian courtship must be brought back to our society and especially the community of believers. Therefore, anyone moving into this ministry will not be allowed to date for the first six months in order that a substantial growth in Christian values and priorities can be attained.

The Bible teaches that God has a perfect

plan for our lives (Prov. 3:5,6; 1 Cor. 2:9) and if we learn to seek Him first that He will cause this plan to come to pass in the best time for Himself (Matt. 6:33,34) and us. The Bible also teaches that we are to stay away from any form of lustful (Matt. 2:28-30) or sensual thinking, behavior (Eph. 5:1-5) or premarital intercourse (Gal. 5:19). Our attraction to an individual should be primarily spiritual and based on God's calling (2 Cor. 6:19) rather than only physical and intellectual.

Marriage for the Christian is to be a life-long commitment. The husband is to love his wife as Christ loves the church (Eph. 5:25) and never divorce her (1 Peter 3:7). Also, a wife is to submit to her husband as she submits to the Lord (Eph. 5:22) and not depart from him (1 Cor. 7:10). This should make marriage a serious and awesome thing to us. It certainly is something that we don't want to rush into. As we can see through these Scriptures, it takes an extremely high degree of Christian maturity and commitment to enter into a marriage relationship. Therefore, the guidelines that we have set forth are four stages of courtship. (This process begins for people who are determined by those in charge to be cooperative and sufficiently mature spiritually.)

1. Special Friends (3 months)—This is a casual time of just getting to know someone you may be interested in with *no heavy* commitments or future plans. You are allowed to sit together at meetings, church, Bible studies and meals. No dating or private conversations will be allowed. You will not be allowed to be alone together.

2. Going Steady (3 months)—This is when both people have gotten to know each other a little and feel mutual leading of God to a deeper and more serious relationship. The rules are the same as special friends with the exception that they could go on dates with another couple from the house.

3. Pre-Engagement (3 months)—This is a time of seriously seeking God's will for marriage with the mutual understanding that either of the couple can back out at any time. Private time of one-half hour a day will be allowed in office. Other rules are same as going steady.

4. Engagement (3 months)—This is a time of making absolutely certain of God's will and preparation for marriage through counseling with a qualified individual. This is also entered into with the understanding that either person can change their mind. Dating and time alone will be allowed.

5. If any of these guidelines are broken, the couple will be set back one or more stages, depending on the seriousness of the situation.

The above rules may sound repressive to most of us relational, middle-class types. I would never want some of the structure mentality we use in the street ministry to influence the entire church. But the beauty of the Body is that we're flexible enough to have the structure in those segments of the Body that need it. In the first six years of this ministry, 20 couples survived these guidelines and wound up marrying. And all but one couple are still together.

The street ministry has endless possibilities. What a shame that the evangelical church is so poorly represented among this target group. The cults are there in full force, flourishing from the response of these spiritually hungry people. If they can become so committed to the counterfeits, imagine the potential for developing genuine Christian disciples from among this target group. Thank God for the work Teen Challenge, the Salvation Army, rescue missions and others are doing. But can you imagine the potential if hundreds of local churches would get involved?

## Chapter 15

# Reaching Middle-Class Families

The suburban church is built on the middle-class family unit—which means dad, mom and child(ren). These people serve on most of the church boards and committees, they teach Sunday School, they participate in the choirs and work in the nurseries. They also finance most of the church's budget.

In the fortress church they are the constant focus of attention. In the church unleashed the tendency may be to neglect them in favor of ministering to the more unusual target groups. Much of what has been said about renewal in the church has advocated abandoning the traditional ministries that have meant so much to the middle-class family unit. One senses a tone of scorn, blaming the middle class for the ills of the church.

We believe, however, that the church unleashed can and should focus much of its ministry on the middle class. In spite of this group's apparent affluence and self-sufficiency, it has some real needs that the church should be attempting to meet.

## A Ministry to Adult Men

One doesn't have to be in the ministry long before he or she realizes that perhaps the most widespread discontentment among men, Christians and non-Christians, is occupational discontent. Studs Terkel wrote the fascinating book, *Working*. In the preface he quotes Nora Watson as having said, "I think most of us are looking for a calling, not a job. . . . Jobs are not big enough for people."[1]

After listening to hours of expression of occupational discontent, Pastor Roger Thompson decided to start a new ministry. The ministry is geared to the Christian who feels like most of the people Terkel interviewed in *Working*—those not happy with their work. I asked Pastor Thompson to introduce the ministry he calls the Tentmakers' Union.

The Tentmakers' Union takes its name from the example of Paul in Acts 18:1-3. Though involved as a tradesman making tents in the secular marketplace, Paul was a militant witness and discipler. In fact, the two key people he met while tentmaking in Philippi, Aquila and Priscilla, later became involved in discipling Apollos.

Tentmaking consumes the greater part of the available time of most men and women. Particularly as we speak about men, the secular work place is a necessary evil. Not only does the typical Christian man lack a strategy for his office or shop, but normally he hates his job with the same intensity as anyone else. This diminished sense of vocation (calling), coupled with the lack of fulfillment that work brings, has left the marketplace a wasteland for Christian witness.

The Tentmakers' Union was born out of just such needs and frustrations. In the summer of 1979 a group of men began to meet on Wednesday mornings for the purpose of encouragement and prayer. These men were all vitally involved in the church, discipleship, Bible study, and had healthy, growing relationships at home. For all intents and purposes, they were models of vibrant Christian men. But as we shared our lives over the next year, a particular theme emerged. We discovered that the single most exasperating element in all these lives was the demand of working in secular businesses. A vast majority of our time was consumed with helping each other make decisions about job changes, job dissatisfactions, employer hassles, and pressure. It became apparent that too few Christian men had any idea of how to fit their faith into the problems of the business world. A ministry was born.

The format of The Tentmakers' Union has been a 6:15 A.M. breakfast meeting. Twice each month, for one hour and fifteen minutes, we meet for fellowship and challenge. Though we periodically consider a different time for meeting, we have stayed with this early morning time for two reasons: (1) it minimizes conflict in the evenings for families, and (2) it assures us of a high interest and commitment. We take the first thirty minutes for breakfast (which is provided at minimal cost) and fellowship. The remainder of the time until 7:30 is then devoted to the topic of the morning.

The Tentmakers' Union operates under the assumption that a man's relationships and his work are linked. If there is pressure in his home life, his work will be affected. If there is pressure at work, his family will feel it. Thus far, however, our experience has shown us that the work place has a greater effect on other areas than vice versa. Men tend to find most of their sense of personal worth from their performance on the job. When there is conflict or frustration every eight-hour day, the home and marriage suffer.

As a result of this assumption about men, our approach has been to emphasize the realities, but also the possibilities, of the marketplace and to offer personal models in specific areas of decision-making. Topics covered include: "The Biblical View of Work," "When Is It Time to Quit?" "Bursting Out of Boredom," "Planning for Your Next Vacation," "Dealing with Temptation," "To Better Love Her," "How to Stay Motivated," "Job Burn-out." All of these have been presented by men within the group and have related these common areas of struggle to the Scripture. As well, we have invited a panel of women to discuss with us how a man can give a Christian witness by his behavior around women on the job.

Balancing all this input has been the periodic sharing of men who have learned and modeled Christian principles under difficult circumstances. One shared how he lost his job because his personal convictions were published in a magazine article. Another expressed poignantly the agony of being indicted by a federal grand jury, admitted his secondhand involvement, and told how he was willing to honestly face the process. Others have simply shared their feelings of burn-out, frustrations with bosses and employees, and struggles about changing jobs. Still others have been very sucessful at building relationships at work, and have given pointers about how to initiate contact.

In all of these related topics we've tried to deal specifically with the unique world of men. Christian men must find a certain degree of fulfillment in both family and work.

Dealing with this area is a matter of balance. On the one hand is the reality that no job will ever satisfy the spiritual hunger and need for fulfillment of men. However, there can be reasonable expectations. Many men need to face the fact that they are looking for total satisfaction at work—a completely unrealistic assumption. These men need to focus on the opportunities for which God has placed them there—opportunities beyond their own enjoyment. Every job will contain its own forms of drudgery and boredom, but that is not necessarily a reason to leave. We find many Christian men moving and quitting without considering the larger reasons for their involvement in the marketplace. Herein lies a great, untapped missionary force.

On the other hand, man is not an ox. He is not meant to slog through his entire life on a treadmill. To men who are afraid to move on in their work life, or who are trapped by "security," the call of God to militance needs to be emphasized. Many men are slaves—well-paid—but slaves nevertheless. Benefits and salaries were never meant to totally determine the will of God. For these men, the call to mission and faith needs to be sounded.

With men changing jobs on an average of every two years, and changing careers at least three times during their working years, the area of sound counsel is taking on an important role. The Tentmakers' Union hopes to develop over the years as a place in which men can be honest about their wishes, pressures, and choices.

The on-the-job Christian is the largest potential missionary force available to the church. It exists with international possibilities as well as with inner-city influence. There is no strata of society, no technical skill, no professional language into which the Christian community has not already penetrated. The task is to mobilize, train, and encourage that missionary force so that it can see, evangelize, and disciple as the apostle Paul did in his tentmaking activities in Corinth.

Following are some resources concerning men's ministries:

Tim Hansel. *When I Relax I Feel Guilty*. Grand Rapids: David C. Cook Publishing Co., 1979.

Wayne E. Oates. *Confessions of a Workaholic*. Nashville: Abingdon Press, 1978.

R. C. Sproul. *Stronger Than Steel*. San Francisco: Harper and Row, 1980.

Jerry White. *Honesty, Morality and Conscience*. Colorado Springs: NavPress Publishing Co.

Jerry E. White and Mary E. White. *Your Job: Survival or Satisfaction*. Grand Rapids: Zondervan Publishing Co., 1976.

J. Christy Wilson, Jr., *Today's Tentmakers, Self-Support: An alternative model for worldwide witness*. Wheaton, IL: Tyndale House Publishers.

### Marriage Enrichment and Money Management

Once again a parachurch ministry has demonstrated that there is a tremendous need most churches are ignoring. Marriage Encounter, which I understand was started by the Roman Catholics and now has several denominational expressions, has simply exploded across the country. The need for marriage enrichment is clear, calling for the constant concern of the church. What can we do?

First, we can schedule regular marriage enrichment retreats. At Bear Valley we attempt to provide an opportunity for couples to get away by having a marriage enrichment weekend each season of the year. These four retreats are limited to ten couples each. We have found an abundance of good materials to use during such weekends. But as Marriage Encounter has demonstrated, perhaps the most valuable thing we can do is to simply give couples time together away from the pressures of the home and job.

We can also hold seminars in the church dealing with those potential problem areas such as money and sex. For example, a couple of years ago Dr. and Mrs. Penner conducted a Sexual Fulfillment[2] seminar for our married couples. The seminar dealt with the touchy areas of sex, tastefully, explicitly and from a Christian point of view. We have also tried to hold occasional seminars on the Christian and money management.

In addition to the things mentioned above, we regularly attempt to carry on the marriage enrichment and money management ministry through sermons and by stocking and promoting quality tapes and books in the church library. Both marriage enrichment and money management are continual areas of high interest to the middle-class Christian couple.

## MOPS—Mothers of Pre-Schoolers

This ministry is aimed at one of the most strategic groups in society—mothers of preschoolers. Who is more important than the person who has the greatest influence in a young child's life? Things are particularly difficult for mothers of young children in our culture. The message they most often hear is, "You have to establish a career to have real independence and fulfillment." Remaining at home these days has come to mean living with the stigma of being second class.

Anyone who has raised children knows that the preschool mother has perhaps the most demanding of all jobs. When Mom opts to stay in the home with a young child rather than using day care, she has assumed the most influential career possible. She is the first "significant other" in a child's life and as a result she often has the greatest input into shaping the child's self-image. A MOPS ministry is a way for the church to say to this important target group of mothers, "You are a special people. Your job is of critical importance."

Susan Kafer initiated the ministry for us in 1972. I asked her to share some of the methodology of this ministry. The following ideas are hers.

The feelings of inadequacy that come with raising small children are the same today as thirty or forty years ago. The questions are the same. Mothers have always wondered whether to toilet train at two or three years of age. Babies have always had illnesses diagnosed as insignificant by doctors but which perplexed the mother. Mothers have always gotten cabin fever when having to remain in the house as chicken pox slowly works its way through each child. Today, though, where does a mother go for the support of friends when all of her neighbors have gone to work?

In days past, often more than one woman lived in a household. Women worked together, cooked together and had their children together. They learned from one another. They also received on-the-job training in parenting skills from their own parents. But these family-learning experiences are no longer available when the immediate family has moved and moved and moved again.

Is there really any question as to why women are running away, physically abusing their children, finding all of their fulfillment outside of the home or turning to alcohol or drugs?

The picture is not a pretty one, but it is sadly true. Contrast that picture with a group of young women meeting in an atmosphere of acceptance, love and concern. MOPS meetings are designed to be a place where young mothers can share, cry, or stomp their feet if need be. Since the nursery is open, they can spend a few hours away from the children, learning to be better mothers and wives. The emphasis is placed on developing personal relationships and recognizing the vitally beautiful role God has planned for them.

The MOPS program normally consists of meetings twice a month.

| 9:30 to 10:00 | Announcements, refreshments, icebreakers |
| 10:00 to 11:00 | Teaching time and small group discussions |
| 11:00 to 12:00 | Crafts |

Very little is needed to begin this ministry but there are a few essentials:

*Facilities*: (1) room for the women to meet for the teaching time and crafts with chairs and tables; (2) rooms for the children where a quality child-care program can be presented. This eventually should become a Sunday School type of program exposing the children to the gospel.

*Finances*: (1) most of the expenses are taken care of by the women (crafts, nursery, etc.); (2) some financial aid can be given in order that MOPS not become a financial burden to mothers who cannot afford such expenses; (3) if nursery is made up of paid workers, some subsidy may be needed for time.

*Nucleus of committed Christian women* (in its beginning stages the MOPS group may be small enough to need only a couple of women in leadership): (1) planning team—sets the policies, makes decisions and sets up the programs; (2) teaching leaders—Titus 2:4 states that the older women should "train the younger women to love their husbands and children"; (3) children's workers— when young mothers are comfortable about their children's care, they themselves become more open to learning situations. The children's quality care and teaching, with take-home materials, will have an additional impact on these families.

The craft program is an important facet of MOPS. It lends a nonthreatening atmosphere in which mothers can discuss the morning's lessons or personal experiences and make friendships. It also provides an opportunity for women to learn skills, use different media and employ creative talents. And it gives busy mothers a chance to make inexpensive gifts and articles for home and family.

Spiritual as well as tangible needs are basically the same in non-Christian as well as Christian women. It becomes an easy matter then for church women to bring their own unchurched friends to MOPS. This effect then tends to snowball as unchurched women bring their own unchurched friends. In this way MOPS acts as an outreach ministry of the church.

MOPS also provides creative avenues of outreach other than regular meetings and children's programs. Brunches a couple of times a year are very special. Dinners for MOPS and their husbands with good food, good music and fun are great opportunities to show Christianity in a different light than some may think of it. Don't be surprised if after a dinner you see young couples at a church service who have never come before.

Newsletters, using the creative talents of the MOPS women, can be written and circulated. Not only are they a means of expression for the women, they are also a teaching tool and advertisement for the ministry of outreach to other young mothers.

Due to the diverse spiritual backgrounds among the women, it is essential to focus on the similarity of their needs from God's perspective. This is accomplished by leading, not prodding, each to recognize her responsibility and also her potential in light of Scripture.

MOPS is not mere Bible study. Modeling and applying God's principles creates an atmosphere for the Holy Spirit to work.

The testimonies of MOPS women are many and varied. Non-Christian women find in MOPS a refuge where they are accepted and loved, and also a place to search and find that which is missing in their own lives. After coming to know the Lord, the new Christian finds in MOPS a place for spiritual growth and Christian relationships. And young churchwomen who have scheduled themselves into days that are too busy, find in MOPS a place to relax and make friends.

In MOPS no one is a spectator. Everyone is asked to participate in some way. Sharing in the workload helps prevent burnout among the leadership and helps the growth of each participant. Young women who would never have dreamed of speaking in front of a group, volunteer to make phone calls, then volunteer for other things and eventually find themselves in leadership roles—mature, confident and competent. They then move into the mainstream of the life of the Body as these qualities flow naturally into the home, the church, and the community.

Some excellent materials have been developed to help churches with a MOPS ministry. You may contact MOPS OUTREACH and request the MOPS handbook and related materials. The address is 5884 Urban Court, Arvada, Colorado 80004.

### Nurseries

When we remodeled our small building we had space to enlarge only two parts of it. It took us no time at all to decide that the largest share of that space should go to the nursery. On top of that we gave our nursery coordinators a blank check. We told them to design the rooms so that they would be the very best for the children. Middle-class moms are normally very touchy about the quality of ministry and cleanliness of the nurseries, and rightly so. Nurseries should not only be clean, but they should be bright and cheery as well.

The nursery is a very important ministry. Paid workers ought to be paid enough so that the church can expect them to do a good job. Volunteers should see the significance of what they're doing.

The church shouldn't hesitate to use its nursery. Since most couples don't like to keep their children with them while they're attending church functions, the nursery should be available. The church also shouldn't hesitate to hire a nursery coordinator. I realize that many people think the nursery should be strictly a volunteer ministry. That's OK if the quality is top-notch. However, if hiring someone will produce a better nursery, the investment will be worth it.

### Youth Programs

One of the recurring themes in the renewal

movement has been, "We're not being effective with our teenagers." The house church, the small church, the church built around small groups, normally have very poor youth ministries. Yet middle-class families often feel more need for help from the church with their teenagers than with any other segment of the family.

A few years ago we were fortunate to add an outstanding youth pastor to our staff. He is responsible for the junior high, high school and college/career, but he works directly with the group we feel is the most strategic—the junior high. Jim has developed a perfect blend of big-group, fun-type stuff that kids love and the small-group, one-on-one attention that begins to build quality Christian commitment in their lives.

One of these quality ministries Jim has developed is the Triad. Kids who desire to enter a discipleship ministry are paired up with an adult. One adult and two junior highers make up a Triad. They get together each week. One week they goof off together, go bowling or out for pizza. The next week they study together, go over their Scripture memory and share their quiet times.

We also have part-time paid workers in our high school and college/career ministries. They in turn have several highly-committed volunteer staff members working with them. At Bear Valley we have found that the strongest youth ministries have always been tied to our traditional congregations. An effective ministry to our middle-class church kids is as necessary as the ministry to the kids on the street. That being the case, we feel we need to do this ministry well.

### The Ministry of Music
Fortunately many middle-class families have a

high appreciation of music. Good music ministers
to them in a significant way. If they are musically
talented they want to be part of a quality choir,
and they want their children to be involved in a
quality music program as well.

At Bear Valley our approach to ministry has
some built-in limitations to the ministry of music.
Since we are committed to small facilities, we obviously can't build a 200-voice choir. While we don't
want to hinder the ministry of music, we feel the
big facility and the massive up-front ministry of a
huge choir simply has too many liabilities for the
church unleashed.

Perhaps nothing creates this spectator-performer mentality in a church as readily as a large,
overpowering ministry of music. If you want to
build a huge church today, the quickest way is to
knock their lights out with powerful, slick musical
presentations. But the good thing about the small
facility is that you simply cannot build the church
around whatever or whoever is up front; the up-
front is too small. Therefore the road to building a
large ministry in a small facility is to unleash the
church into ministry.

Admittedly when it comes to the ministry of
music, the church unleashed, housed in modest
facilities, will have some built-in drawbacks. But
working within those limitations, we ought to
have the very best ministry we possibly can. When
budgets are submitted for our choirs (which start
for children three years old and above) we expect
the directors to ask for the music, the instruments, the workshops, whatever they need to do
the best job possible.

It's interesting to observe the different musical
needs of our various congregations. The informal
congregations do not require any finances for

their music "program." There is no choir; people bring their own guitars and other instruments; they sometimes write their own music—things are pretty laid-back. There isn't a lot of rehearsal or materials needed. But the traditional congregations need a substantial budget plus large numbers of people who spend hours in rehearsal.

It would be a great mistake to try to change the approach of the ministry of music in the traditional congregations to make them more like the alternative congregations. We could say the money and hours of time need to be channeled into working with refugees or people in prison. But that would be to neglect the legitimate needs of many people in our church. The church unleashed need not choose between ministering to the middle class or to the target groups—it can do both.

### The Navigator 2:7 Discipleship Ministry

When new believers enter your church, somehow they need to be helped to grow. We found the Navigator 2:7 Discipleship Ministry an excellent tool.

For years the Navigators, a parachurch ministry working primarily with the military, collegians and business people, have had great success with discipleship ministries among the middle class. In the early seventies some of the Navigator staff began to work on a discipleship course designed especially for the local church. They took the strategy and the tools that have proved so effective over the years and packaged them into a workable discipleship program for the church.

One of the finest methods I know for raising up lay leaders is the use of *The 2:7 Series* produced by NavPress (the name comes from Colossians 2:7). For eight years it was field-tested and revised. Bear

Valley was one of the first three churches involved in that field-testing and the results were excellent from the beginning. Many other discipleship programs are available to help new believers grow and mature. Navigators' 2:7 series is one of the best. (Write to NavPress Publishing Co., P.O. Box 20, Colorado Springs, CO 80901.)

### The King's Art Guild

The King's Art Guild began as three Christian artists met informally to paint and share together. Sensing a growing frustration in other artists who were exploring the significance of their gifts and talents, the three artists expanded their group into a ministry under the sponsorship of Bear Valley.

Writings by Francis Shaeffer, H. R. Rookmaaker and others have challenged Christian artists to take their unique role in Christ's kingdom more seriously. They have begun to understand that their creativity is a gift from a creative God to be used and developed for His glory. Artists have an important work to do as part of the Body of Christ.

Our vision for the King's Art Guild is based on these two thoughts (1) glorifying God is the most important reason for art; and (2) art can play an important part in influencing our culture for Jesus Christ. Art does not have to be "religious" in subject matter to accomplish either of these objectives.

Throughout history we see that artists have been influenced by the philosophies of their day and have in turn influenced public opinion to accept or reject those ideas. The arts are the stage where philosophies are tossed around and discussed; the world is the audience who watches and absorbs those ideas. We are convinced that public opinion, whether right or wrong, has historically been shaped by the arts, including visual arts, music, writing, theater, dance, and in our own time, movies and television. Who then is responsible for shaping public opinion? Artists are—artists in *all* these fields. Who has the greatest potential for influencing our culture for Jesus Christ? Christian artists. Have Christian artists been meeting that challenge? No, many are being told that art is a nice little hobby to pursue after they have finished soul-winning for the day. What a tremendous waste of God-given potential!

The King's Art Guild was formed so that Christian artists might individually and collectively glorify God and have a positive impact on our culture. We don't worry about the group's size, which may remain small, because we know how many times history has been changed by the actions of a small group of people. One of the best examples of this is the French Impressionists, whose art we appreciate and enjoy. Of course we can never agree with their philosophy; but they were a small group of artists who all knew each other and got together to discuss what they believed and wanted to accomplish. They were misunderstood and rejected by the society of their day, but they supported each other. Their work reflected their philosophy of art and life which ultimately influenced their society and the world. If a handful of French artists, driven by a humanistic spirit, could change the course of art history, what could a handful of Christian artists, united and led by the power of the Holy Spirit, do? We can't even dream of what we might accomplish.

We attempt to have this influence in the following ways:

1. Strive constantly to improve our work so that it meets and exceeds the world's standard of quality.

2. Work to get individual Christian artists into art galleries and museums.

3. Exhibit as a group in churches, businesses, sidewalk shows, etc. to let our light and testimony shine out to the world.

4. Explore and understand our own beliefs and our Christian perspective of art so that our work has greater depth and insight. We don't want our work to become nothing more than religious propaganda.

5. Help the Christian community to recognize the importance and potential of all the arts. We have put together a slide presentation which we show at various churches when invited to do a program.

6. Work in cooperation with other Christian arts groups, such as writing, music, drama and dance groups.

7. Encourage, educate and inform Christian artists throughout the U.S. and Canada through our newsletter.

Monthly meetings aim toward personal growth and fellowship with a variety of activities including speakers and discussions on a Christian perspective of art, slide presentations, lectures and workshops on art techniques, matting and framing, exhibiting in galleries, and anything which encourages growth as Christian artists.

There are four basic requirements for membership in the Guild:

First, since the guild is a nondenominational group, a prospective member must *share his personal testimony* with someone on the leadership staff to be certain that he has committed his life to

Jesus Christ. Non-Christians are welcome as visitors but may not become members.

Second, he must commit to the *financial support* of the guild through annual dues and commissions. A prospective member must agree to pay the guild a ten percent commission on works sold through guild shows and exhibits to help fund the guild's activities.

Third, he must commit to *regular attendance* of monthly meetings.

Fourth, since the guild is a ministry more than a social organization, a prospective member must agree to do *something to support the group's activities*. He may choose to help with the newsletter mailings, make coffee at meetings, serve as librarian for the resource materials, help put up and take down shows, serve on the leadership team, speak at other churches, or one of many other activities. In this way the administration of the group is divided among everyone, rather than asking a few to do everything. The guild doesn't try to replace the spiritual training of an individual's church, nor does it attempt to be a substitute for artistic training gained in classes and schools. Instead it attempts to combine the two into an integrated, healthy perspective of art and Christianity.

### Developing an Unleashed Attitude Toward the Middle Class

Earlier it was said that a major problem with the church in the United States was its almost total preoccupation with the middle-class family unit. The contention was that we needed to think beyond traditional ministries and approaches. And it is true that we need to learn how to contact, share the gospel, and effectively minister to the growing segments of our cities that are outside the middle class.

The intention, however, need not imply that we stop thinking about creative new ways to minister to the middle class. At Bear Valley, our MOPS (Mothers of Pre-Schoolers) group has drawn women primarily from suburbia. So has our ministry built around ceramics. A while back a woman happened to donate a kiln to the church. Some imaginative people saw the possibilities and established regular times when those interested in ceramics could come to the church and work with clay. It has turned into an effective means of outreach as people invited their neighbors to join them at the ceramics class. With that natural bridge, relationships have been formed that are bringing people to Jesus and His church.

Another specialized ministry that appeals to the middle class is the health-care ministry. This ministry conducts aerobic exercise classes, has started a blood bank, brought in Red Cross people to teach teenagers a baby-sitting course, and has conducted workshops on cardiopulmonary resuscitation. It also sponsored a class for new wives on "Cooking for Two." Other health activities take place in the home—meals for the sick, allergy shots, bed-baths, shopping for those confined, and so on. The objective of the health-care ministry is to serve the church by helping people care for their physical as well as spiritual needs.

A fairly new ministry that is already paying rich dividends to some of our middle-class families is a wilderness backpacking ministry. As usual, this ministry began as the brainchild of one of our lay people. The first summer it was suggested we field-tested it with a couple of small father-son groups and some borrowed equipment. The results were so positive that we invested a few thousand dollars worth of equipment and the following summer expanded the trips from two to six. So far these trips have been father-son or coed junior high and senior high. In the future we plan to run family, father-daughter, mother-son, and numerous other combinations.

When we talk about the church unleashed at Bear Valley we mean a ministry that includes traditional and new ministries to the middle class as well as to target groups. We believe the local church can be effective with all the diverse ministry possibilities of the city and at the same time not neglect suburbia and its needs.

### Notes

1. Studs Terkel, *Working* (New York: Avon Books, 1975), preface.
2. Clifford and Joyce Penner, *The Gift of Sex*, (Waco, TX: Word Books, 1981).

## Chapter 16

# Developing a Global Vision

There is a church in our area that was started with fifty percent of its budget committed to missions. Over the years that church has poured large amounts of money into overseas missions and has seen several of its members become foreign missionaries. Like so many churches, its greatest strength has been foreign missions. But over the past ten years this church has experienced a steady decline. Although they have made a courageous effort to maintain the original fifty percent commitment, at this point it is no longer possible.

But this church still has a sizeable mission budget. The impact of the church on its own community and the metropolitan area, however, has become negligible. This church illustrates one of the dangers of a strong foreign mission emphasis—it may detract from the urgency to build a strong local outreach. On the other hand, a danger of the church unleashed is that it may get so involved in local ministries it loses its worldwide vision. What can we do?

### Constantly Teach the Acts 1:8 Progression

"But you will receive power when the Holy Spirit comes on you; and you will be my witnesses in Jerusalem, and in all Judea and Samaria, and to the ends of the earth" (Acts 1:8).

The commitment to missions begins in our Jerusalem, but it certainly doesn't end there. We are responsible to keep reaching out until we have a part in the great commission around the world. As we do so, however, it is important to emphasize our primary responsibility to our Jerusalem. People must grasp the fact that the church *is* missions; the church just doesn't support missions.

Before we support someone else outside our church to do a ministry we need to ask ourselves if we should instead be supporting someone from within to do that ministry. The answer to that question is often yes, when the ministry is a local one. But when the request is to help overseas it may not be practical for us to try to do it ourselves.

Recently at Bear Valley we funded a Here's Life Training Center in Sweden sponsored by Campus Crusade for Christ. Our role in this effort was to pray and send money. But if there had been any practical way we could have accomplished the same thing directly as a church we would have done so because we feel the primary role of the church is to do missions, not merely to support them. And herein lies the problem with so many churches like the one described at the beginning of this chapter. The people in such churches too often come to see their primary role as being the prayer supporters and financiers of mission projects.

## Provide a Solid Home Base for Those Going Overseas

Once the ministry at Jerusalem is firmly established we need to look beyond our home-base. We are continually looking for opportunities to get our people out of Denver on mission projects. Sending our teenagers to rural Colorado towns or into Mexico has given them a taste of frontline ministry away from the home-base.

The most exciting thing we have done in the area of direct missions, however, has gone beyond our city, state or neighboring country. Thus far we have sent teams ranging from eight to twenty-two people to Korea, France, Norway, and Spain. These partnership trips have been made in coordination with Baptist missionaries overseas. However it is done, it is beneficial to encourage our people to go overseas for short-term missions.

Maybe we can direct them toward Greater Europe Mission or Operation Mobilization or one of the dozens of other groups sending short-termers overseas. Regardless of how it is done, the message that we encourage everyone to go overseas is a healthy one.

The benefits from lay people spending short terms (two weeks to a year) overseas are many. First, we're convinced the churches overseas benefit. Whether they benefit from one of our college kids working on the dorms of a European Bible institute, or another one of our people handing out tracts and witnessing in the streets, either way the work of Christ in that country is helped.

No matter how much the foreign church is helped, however, it's likely our church benefits the most. Once people have experienced being a foreign missionary it's easier for them to see themselves as "full-time" workers back home. It's a maturing, stretching experience for the average Christian to give his testimony through an interpreter or to witness in the streets of a foreign city.

Another direct benefit of being overseas is an appreciation of what it's like to be in a foreign culture. Some of our most effective international student and refugee workers have been those who have gone on one of these short mission trips. They have come back with something most Americans lack, an empathy for the foreigner.

In addition, nearly everyone returns deeply grateful for the strength of Christianity in America. We tend to take our incredible resources lightly until we've been with Christians who have very little Christian radio, television, books, Sunday School materials, colleges, seminaries. In fact you name the resource and chances are good that the church overseas does not have it.

Seeing the lack of resources has given people in our church a deep desire to invest more heavily overseas. That means sending money to special projects that will assist churches abroad. It also means sending people on short-term mission trips, plus supporting more and more career missionaries.

It's interesting that if we follow the Acts 1:8 progression it may mean an initial emphasis on the home base, but in the long run we contribute to the Lord's work in neighboring cities, states and countries as well.

Now you know how we at Bear Valley have unleashed our church. Much of the ministry described in this book did not become part of the church quickly. We have attempted to learn the art of practicing "relaxed concern." The needs of the city are overwhelming. Of course if a church focuses within its fortress, the needs outside will always remain invisible. What you don't know doesn't hurt you (or stir you to action). But once you begin to look and see as He sees, you'll probably be tempted to try to move too fast. It may seem imperative at first to try guilt-motivation to get people involved in ministry. But since that seldom works, you may then feel obliged to conclude that people just aren't interested in being involved in front-line ministries. But this isn't true. We must be patient and allow God to move people in His own time. At Bear Valley during the 1970s, a base for major ministry to the city has been patiently, painstakingly built.

Now in the 1980s our active fellowship is 1,000 strong. Individuals and groups are specializing in ministries to street people, international students, ex-convicts, the elderly, mothers of preschoolers, writers, artists, kids who are wards of the state, singles and refugees. There are more target groups we would like to work with, such as the cults, unchurched teens, mothers of preschoolers in apartment complexes, homosexuals, people in prisons and jails, unchurched businessmen, ex-prostitutes, unwed mothers—and undoubtedly God has even more specialized ministries in mind than we have been able to think of.

Our objectives for the 1980s include more than adding target-group ministries and sponsoring mission churches. We would like to influence churches across the country to think as normally about ministries to international students and ex-convicts as they do about Sunday School and choir. We would also like to be influenced by churches who are reaching the cities' target groups. We want to share ideas and dreams with hundreds of other churches that are ministering effectively in their communities. We would especially like to hear from those of you who are building major ministries in modest facilities.

The church unleashed will become the "church visible" in the city. Visible, not because of huge facilities or television programs, but because everywhere people go they will encounter Christians who care. There is not a segment of the city that we do not have the resources to reach. We in the local churches do not need to depend on everyone else to grow arms of ministry for us; we can grow our own. We do not have to be that shriveled-up octopus I mentioned earlier. We can truly be the radiant Bride of Christ.